PRAISE FOR

DRINKING WITH MEN

"A witty homage to pubs and bars and the regulars who call them home."
—*O, The Oprah Magazine*

"[Schaap] describes the unusual camaraderie among bar 'regulars' with poignant specificity. It's a cozy, intimate pleasure to go belly-to-bar with her."
—*Entertainment Weekly*

"With focused premise and expansive feeling . . . [and] very smart assessments of a mode of being that's not given the credit it deserves. *Drinking with Men* would pair very well this time of year with a well-aged whiskey and a handful of peanuts."
—*The Boston Globe*

"A wonderfully funny and openhearted book from a generous, charismatic writer. . . . [Schaap is] a born storyteller . . . There's no substitute for the kind of community you can find in a good tavern. And no American writer can explain it better than Rosie Schaap."
—*NPR*

"Rosie Schaap's *New York Times* column on the pleasures of drinking has always been—like the best bartenders—funny, smart, and slightly bawdy. This memoir is also all those things—and there's no hangover."
—*W Magazine*

"Beautifully rendered."
—*The Daily Beast*

"Funny, smart-as-hell, moving."
—*Salon*

"Witty . . . A vivid study of both Schaap's life in bars, often as one of the few women regulars, and a gimlet-eyed exploration of modern bar culture."
—*Chicago Tribune*

"Schaap warmly toasts the urge so many of us share to find a spot where everybody knows your name." —*People*

"[Schaap] has a way with words, writing about her experiences in the bars of her life in a heartfelt, honest, and relatable way. I would like to request a drink pairing with each chapter." —*The Atlantic Wire*

"Phenomenal . . . Schaap is an expert storyteller." —*Food & Wine*

"Ms. Schaap has a gift for camaraderie—and excellent taste in booze." —*The New York Observer*

"Pour yourself a double and let Schaap's writing amuse and enchant you." —*BookPage*

"Schaap is a gifted storyteller." —*Time Out Chicago*

"Witty, compassionate . . . a meditation on learning how to drink well, wisely, and with eyes wide open. . . . If you want an elegy to good bars and a stiff drink, Schaap has you covered." —*Full Stop*

"Schaap brings a poet's touch to her memoir, which brims with insight and wisdom." —Jimmy Breslin

"This book will be a classic. There is so much joy in this book! It's a great, comforting, wonderful, funny, inspiring, moving memoir about community and belief and the immense redemptive powers of alcohol drunk properly."
—Kate Christensen, author of *In the Drink* and *The Great Man*

"There are bar stories and there are coming-of-age stories. And then there is Rosie Schaap's thoughtful and funny chronicle that reminds us of all the drinks, dives, and deep conversations that helped make us who we are. This is a wise, engaging memoir."
—Wendy McClure, author of *The Wilder Life* and *I'm Not the New Me*

DRINKING
with
MEN

ROSIE SCHAAP

RIVERHEAD BOOKS
New York

RIVERHEAD BOOKS
Published by the Penguin Group
Penguin Group (USA) LLC
375 Hudson Street, New York, New York 10014, USA

USA • Canada • UK • Ireland • Australia • New Zealand • India • South Africa • China

penguin.com

A Penguin Random House Company

The Library of Congress has catalogued the Riverhead hardcover edition as follows:

Schaap, Rosie.
Drinking with men / Rosie Schaap.
p.   cm.
ISBN 978-1-59448-711-8 (hardback)
1. Schaap, Rosie.   2. Bars (Drinking establishments).   I. Title.
HV5137.S33   2013
362.292092—dc23
[B]
2012030405

First Riverhead hardcover edition: January 2013
First Riverhead trade paperback edition: January 2014
Riverhead trade paperback ISBN: 978-1-59463-231-0

PRINTED IN THE UNITED STATES OF AMERICA

10 9 8 7 6 5 4 3 2 1

Cover design by Janet Hansen
Cover photograph © Ryan McVay / Getty Images
Book design by Susan Walsh

Some names and identifying characteristics have been changed to protect
the privacy of the individuals involved.

Penguin is committed to publishing works of quality and integrity.
In that spirit, we are proud to offer this book to our readers;
however, the story, the experiences, and the words
are the author's alone.

For Ma, and for Frank

Time is never called in my recurring
dream of pubs.

—CIARAN CARSON, *Last Night's Fun*

CONTENTS

DRINKING

with

MEN

INTRODUCTION

>10<

Thirteen thousand hours.

That's a rough estimate, scratched out on the cocktail napkin in front of me, of how much time I've spent in bars. An indelible reckoning.

Many people would say that every one of those hours was wasted, but not me. I wouldn't change a moment—not even the time I nearly got clocked by a barstool turned projectile in the midst of an altercation between two grizzled old punks, nor the evening a seemingly innocuous, if inebriated, couple all but forced me to referee their debate about whether they should stay together or break up. (For the record: I thought they were a perfect match, and advised them to give it another shot.) I've come of age in bars, and they've given me as much of an education as college did, and have fostered many of my strongest friendships. That could be why a certain type of bar—small, welcoming, with a lively chorus of voices and the house lights turned down to a warm glow—will exert a gravitational pull, compelling me to return one night after the other, and often twice on Sundays.

But my attraction to bars is less governed by the laws of physics than it is by the rules of romance: I prefer one bar at a time. When it comes to where I drink, I'm a serial monogamist. Still, although loyalty is upheld as a virtue, bar regularhood—the practice of drinking in a particular establishment so often that you become known by, and bond with, both the bartenders and your fellow patrons—is often looked down upon in a culture obsessed with health and work. But despite what we are often told, being a regular isn't synonymous with being a drunk; regularhood is much more about the camaraderie than the alcohol. Sharing the joys of drink and conversation with friends old and new, in a comfortable and familiar setting, is one of life's most unheralded pleasures.

And yes, that goes for women, too. Or it should, anyway. If regularhood is considered suspect behavior, then female regularhood is doubly so. In many parts of the world, women just don't go into bars alone. Even in comparatively less patriarchal societies, such as our own, a solitary woman at a bar is a curiosity, a wonderment to be puzzled over. And even in New York, where all things seem possible, as a bar regular who happens to be female, I am something of an anomaly. Regularhood is still predominantly the province of men.

I've been going into bars since the age of fifteen. Certainly in my youth I knew that patronizing bars was unusual

behavior—but I figured that was due to my age, not my gender. There was the excitement of getting one over and getting
served, of trying to fit in, unquestioned, with grown-ups in
their natural habitat. But as I got older and that thrill abated,
what I discovered in bars was much richer. As a regular, I
have found friendship, comfort, and community. Mostly, I've
found that fellowship in the company of men. Relations
between the sexes at bars are often perceived as predatory
and dangerous. But I did not look to bars for a place to hook
up; I looked to bars for a place to belong.

In 1936, *Vogue* editor Marjorie Hillis counseled readers of
her single-girl guide *Live Alone and Like It.* "It is not incor-
rect for a woman to go alone into any bar she can get into,"
she wrote, "but we don't advise it . . . if you must have your
drink, you can have it in a lounge or restaurant, where you
won't look forlorn or conspicuous." I find it remarkable—
and a little depressing—that nearly eighty years later, ideas
identical to hers still seem deeply internalized by many
women. "I just don't feel comfortable walking into a bar
alone," a friend once told me. "Like everyone's looking at me
and feeling sorry for me. Like there's something wrong with
girls who go drinking by themselves."

For better or worse, I've seldom worried about who's
looking at me or not looking at me, or about what they might
or might not be thinking. But I have noticed a pattern: Every
time I've fallen hard for a bar, I've invited my best girlfriends
to join me there for a drink, meet my fellow regulars, soak

up the ambience that I found so appealing. Invariably, they
like it. They have a good time. But, unlike me, they have no
particular interest in returning the next night, or the next, or
the ones that follow. Not only does the idea of becoming a
regular at a bar hold no allure for them, they are also often
puzzled by my enduring bar-love. But they have come to
admire my ability to integrate, to talk to anyone, to be one of
the guys.

In his very funny 1935 tract *Her Foot Is on the Brass
Rail*, the humorist and newspaperman Don Marquis laments
the post-Prohibition presence of women in bars. For men,
there was "no longer any escape, no harbor or refuge . . .
where the hounded male may seek his fellow and strut his
stuff, safe from the atmosphere and presence of femininity."
In my experience these concerns have been beside the point;
if anything, my chronic regularhood has made me assimilate
into a largely male culture, not change it—except by the fact
that I am part of it.

Regardless of my gender, a bar is my safe haven, my
breathing space. Knowing how to read a bar helps. My favorites have never been big, rowdy sports bars teeming with tes-
tosterone or trendy spots featuring cutting-edge cocktails,
but intimate, friendly neighborhood places where relation-
ships with other regulars—and bartenders—have the right
conditions to take hold, and where my instincts tell me it's
a safe space to be a woman in a bar. At its best, bar culture
is both civilized and civilizing, and at the end of a long,

stressful day, I know I can head to my local and the bartender will know exactly what I want—often whiskey, occasionally a mixed drink, but usually these days red wine in a tumbler, as a stem is too much bother—and will set it down before me, ask me about my day, listen to me vent. And instantly, I relax. I remember to exhale.

And it's not just the whiskey or the wine or the martini, though of course they're part of it. It's the atmosphere, the familiarity, the ritual, the community. At the bar, my friends and I greet one another with hugs and pats on the back, catch up on one another's lives (How's the new job? Did your brother move out of your apartment yet? How was your trip back home? Is your mother out of the hospital?), discuss Premier League transfer rumors (Will Tottenham ever get a world-class forward?) and other news of the day, and we all start to feel so much better, so quickly, even if we hadn't really been feeling so bad to begin with.

It seems to me that someone ought to defend the great tradition of regularhood, of passing hours and days and years drinking and talking and laughing in bars. And it's time someone advocated for equal regularhood rights for women everywhere. It might as well be me, a woman with a quarter of a century of devoted bar-going under her belt. Along the way, I'll chronicle my quest for the perfect local haunt, a journey that's taken me from the bar car on the Metro-North railroad to a beloved Dublin pub, and from an expats' haven in New York City to a neighborhood institution in Montreal.

From one bar to the next, I've had the good fortune to drink with painters, cabdrivers, lawyers, ironworkers, professors, musicians, craftsmen, chefs, electricians, poets, and even a tugboat captain. And lately my regular status has led me back to the other side of the bar, serving friends and neighbors at the cozy local pub right around the corner.

More than anywhere else—home, school, or work—bars are where I've figured out how to relate to others and how to be myself. They've not only shaped my identity, they've shaped my point of view—one that is profoundly optimistic about human kindness despite a healthy dose of skepticism. And I challenge anyone who becomes a regular at their neighborhood bar not to feel the same way.

Not long ago, I was talking with a young woman who has lived just a few doors away from one of my favorite bars for more than a year. Like many of her peers in their early twenties, she'd rather go to clubs than bars—especially not neighborhood bars with no complicated cocktails, no hipster cachet, no cute boys anywhere near her age. But she's stopped in a couple times and acknowledged its earthy charm. I asked her if she knew a particular bartender. Mmm, he sounded familiar, but she never got his name. "Go in and introduce yourself," I advised her. "Get to know him. And get to know everyone else who works there, too. And the regulars."

Even if she'd never become a regular there herself, I explained, this was still her corner bar. Being neighborly is a good thing in itself; it also comes in handy. If some night someone was walking down the street a little too close behind her, this is where she'd duck in and be looked after until any danger, real or imagined, had passed. This is where they'd sign for her FedEx package when she wasn't home. This is where she could leave that extra set of keys in case she ever locked herself out of her apartment. And this is where, if she ever happened to be really sad and really broke and really in need of a drink, they'd give her one—and people to talk to, too—and they'd know she'd be good for it, someday.

You can drink anywhere, I told her. You can drink at home. But a good bar? It's more than a place to have a few pints or shots or cocktails. It is much more than the sum of its bottles and bar stools, its glassware and taps and neon beer signs. It's more like a community center, for people—men and women—who happen to drink.

1.

BAR CAR PROPHECY

The Metro-North New Haven Line

In 1986, when I was fifteen, I discovered the bar car on the Metro-North New Haven Line—a dingy, crowded, badly ventilated chamber where commuters drank enough to get a decent buzz going, told dirty jokes, and chain-smoked. These were my kind of people. I liked my friends at school—mostly pothead misfits like me—but these were adults, and, right or wrong, I liked to think of myself as one of them. And even though in my memory the whole place is clouded by a sort of grimy yellow film, it was my kind of joint.

My mother had moved us—herself, my brother, me, a shih tzu, a Lhasa apso, a cat, and a parrot—from Greenwich Village to the suburbs a couple of years earlier for many reasons, but partly, I think, in a desperate bid to make a normal kid of me. It didn't work. I became a druggie, a Deadhead, a reasonably resourceful truant, a small-time delinquent. But I was not without ambition. I wanted to be a mystic.

Once a week, I got a reprieve from my suburban exile. After school every Thursday, I took the train from Westport,

Connecticut, to Manhattan's Grand Central Terminal to see my psychoanalyst. I'd been going since eighth grade and I'd come to enjoy it; the fifty-minute sessions made me feel like the featured guest on a talk show. It helped that my shrink sounded a lot like Dick Cavett.

Except on the few occasions when my mother had called him, crying, after finding a bong in my closet ("It's not mine! I swear! I was just holding that for a friend! It's decorative!") or a roach clip in a jacket pocket ("Oh, that? It's for holding papers together!") and demanded that he submit me to another drug test, I looked forward to seeing my shrink week after week, Thursday after Thursday. Besides, I could pocket the round-trip cab fare Ma gave me to get to his office from Grand Central and back. It was just enough for a dime bag of pot, and I didn't mind having a little time to walk the city streets alone. It was good for thinking.

But from the moment I first stumbled into the bar car after one of our appointments, my return trip to Westport became the best part of my Thursday visits. I liked the company of grown-ups, especially strangers. With them, I found it easy to feel smart and funny and interesting. Easier than it was with my peers.

I first discovered this one summer, years earlier, when I was eight or so and my family was vacationing on Fire Island. Ma sent me to borrow a skillet from the neighbors, a bunch of thirty-somethings in a shared rental. They were lounging on an L-shaped white couch and seemed to get a kick out of everything I said, even the word *skillet*. I wasn't even sure what the word meant until a tall, tanned woman handed me a heavy frying pan with flared sides. I thanked her and turned to leave. But they weren't ready to let me go. They had questions: Who was I? What grade was I in? What was I *into*?

I was astonished by their interest. I sat myself down on a puffy ottoman and asked if they wanted to hear a joke. Did they ever. "So this Jewish American Princess married an Indian chief. Guess what they named their baby?" I paused. "Whitefish." It's a terrible joke. I'd heard my mother tell it to one of her friends. I didn't exactly get it. But those grown-ups, sitting there drinking wine, tumbled off the big white couch, laughing. And I felt like a superstar.

That's not how I felt in the bar car. Surrounded by its regulars, mostly men in wrinkled suits and loosened neck-ties, I felt almost invisible. But I liked listening to them. They were not like the silent, unsociable commuters in the regular cars who napped, read, or reviewed spreadsheets. No, the people in the bar car crowd drank beer or Scotch, laughed loudly, talked fast, and always seemed happy to see one another. They were a tribe, and I wanted in. On the surface, we had little in common: they were mostly male, mostly much older, mostly professionals. I was none of those things. Yet I felt an affinity; here, among these hard-drinking commuting men, in some way I felt that maybe I could be myself. Still, I didn't dare belly up to the bar and order myself a beer;

there was no way the weary, wary, seen-it-all Metro-North crew would serve me. I needed a point of entry.

The night I pulled my tarot cards from my backpack and gave myself a reading, right there in the bar car, I accidentally found just what I was looking for. I'd been studying *The Pictorial Key to the Tarot*, a 1910 primer by Arthur Edward Waite—an English weirdo fairly typical of his day who, like Aleister Crowley, had belonged to the Hermetic Order of the Golden Dawn. I had read that Jimmy Page was into Crowley and the Golden Dawn and all that, so it had to be a good thing. I had cultivated a look that fell somewhere on a spectrum between Madame Blavatsky and Janis Joplin: gauzy Indian dresses, batik caftans, chunky silver rings on my fingers (more delicate ones on my toes), glass beads and colorful embroidery floss woven into my long messy hair. From way back in my mother's closet I had appropriated a paisley head scarf shaped a bit like a turban, shot through with glittery metallic thread and adorned with ruby-red rhinestones and golden tear-shaped studs. A silver pentagram with an amethyst in the middle hung from a black silk cord around my neck, coming to rest on my solar plexus, where, according to the salesman in the New Age bookstore where I bought it, its power would be most effectively transmitted throughout my chakra system.

My tarot cards smelled of patchouli oil and sandalwood incense, tobacco and marijuana smoke, and I kept them safe in one of those fuzzy purple Crown Royal whiskey bags. As I shuffled the deck, I focused my energy on a question I wanted the cards to answer, and then began to lay them out in the Celtic Cross pattern I'd learned from Waite's book. First, the significator: the proxy, the card that stood for me. Then the card that "crossed" me, signifying the things that blocked my path. Next the card that "crowned" me, representing my ideals and aims. And so on and so on, until I'd laid out the tenth and final card, which would reveal the answer to my question.

By then, a small crowd had gathered around me. When I finished, a woman asked if I'd give *her* a reading. It was the first time someone in the bar car had spoken to me without wanting to see my ticket. She asked what I charged. I hadn't thought about that. I mulled it over and told her I thought it was kind of bad mojo to take money for readings—but I was cool with bartering, and I wouldn't mind a beer. She didn't ask how old I was.

Her reading was good, loaded with cards from the cups suit—abundant and comforting—and earthy, practical pen-tacles. I had good news for her. Yes, I said with certainty, she would thrive at her new job. She might even get a promotion soon. She perked up—and discreetly got me that beer, which I tucked behind my back and nursed furtively.

Suddenly it was like a divination marathon. I must have done five readings in an hour. And the more I read, the more confident I grew. I found my voice; a routine took shape. As I set down the cards, I'd sing Neil Young's "After the Gold

Rush" quietly, almost under my breath. *Well, I dreamed I saw the silver spaceships flying in the yellow haze of the sun . . .* Then I'd give the whole pattern an initial once-over and look solemnly into the questioner's eyes. "The cards are here to guide us," I'd say in a voice an octave lower than my own, "but what they tell us is not carved in stone, not written in blood. *You* have the power to change any of this." I believed that. And here were all these grown-ups—accountants, lawyers, executives—hanging on my every word.

I felt pretty good when I got home that night, with a couple of cans of warm beer in my backpack and the satisfying shock of newly acquired power. I brought my cards to school that week and practiced on friends, sitting cross-legged in a carpeted hallway near the cafeteria. And as soon as school let out, I'd hurry home, slam my bedroom door behind me, put on Led Zeppelin's fourth record—*ZoSo*, the one with "Stairway to Heaven" and "The Battle of Evermore," the latter a song I'd play three or four or five times in a row, for there is no finer accompaniment to girly adolescent magic than Sandy Denny's voice—light a stick of incense, take my cards out, and practice some more. This was no joke. Huge and mysterious forces were at work. The cards had power. The cards knew stuff. The cards understood things that even my shrink didn't get.

The next week, after therapy, I stood in front of a mirror in a women's restroom at Grand Central and fitted the paisley head scarf onto my head before boarding the train. And then my fortune-telling-for-alcohol scheme began in earnest. Again, I settled into the bar car and gave myself a reading. And again, a cluster of commuters assembled around me. I felt like I'd cracked a code. They'd sit down next to me and listen obediently: "When you shuffle the cards, put your energy into them. Focus. Concentrate on your question," I instructed them. "The cards will *know* if you're doing this halfheartedly."

This continued for weeks, and out of it I got plenty of beer, a couple of books, and a pair of silver earrings. That, and the undivided attention of all these adults. I'd explain what each position in the Celtic Cross meant, the significance of casting more cups than swords, more wands than pentacles. If someone's reading turned up an unusually high number of major arcana cards (the first twenty-two in the deck, including the Magician, the Moon, the Devil, etc.), I'd go quiet for a moment before I disclosed to him how much power that foretold—and urged him to use that power responsibly, for the greater good.

It didn't take long for me to figure out something that Waite didn't mention in his book: Reading the person was as important as reading the pictures on the cards. I never asked them their names, and I never told them mine—not my real one, anyway. Yet time after time, as I arranged the cards, as I laid out their destinies on a grimy laminated table sticky with liquor and blistered by cigarette burns, complete strangers would drop intimate clues about their lives, their jobs, their

families. More than once, a wingtip-wearing banker or bro-
ker confided in me that he'd taken acid and sloshed around
in the mud at Woodstock and felt very connected to the
energy of the universe. I'd nod and say something like,
"That's awesome, man. I wish *I'd* been there." They had lived
through the sixties, when I had not yet been born. I think for
some of them it was as if I'd materialized before their eyes
like some ghost from their youth come back to answer questions about their future.

Of course, there were people in the bar car who paid me
no mind, and others who made their skepticism known. But
I was dismissive of the nonbelievers and the cynics. They
were out of touch, and that was their loss. Still, one heckler
in the crowd made me nervous. I couldn't pinpoint his age—
midthirties, I guessed. He was a broad-shouldered, thick-
necked guy with a beer gut, strawberry blond hair, and a big
ruddy face. He looked like a distant Kennedy cousin, maybe,
or an overgrown, superannuated frat boy. And did he have a
mouth on him, deploying the F-word as a noun, verb, and
adjective in one sentence, and then the next and the next
and the next, like artillery fire.

This guy was always drunker and louder than anyone
else. Once, he cupped his hands into a makeshift megaphone
and sort of stage-shouted at me, something like "The sixties
are over, get a life!" It was pretty stupid, but it still rattled me
in the middle of a reading and disrupted the flow. And as

much as I basked in my bar car celebrity, I dreaded seeing that guy.

One Thursday, after I'd already served a few of my patrons, he half staggered, half swaggered over to me. "All right," he said. "This is total bullshit. But go ahead. Do mine." He plunked himself down across from me, his knees a little too close, sweat beading on his forehead. I wanted to tell him to go away. I wanted to tell him that his unwillingness to believe would insult the spirits that governed the cards and make them uncooperative. But I figured he'd call me out. That he'd call me a chicken. So instead, I said okay. I kept my cool and started my spiel: "Shuffle. Focus. Give the cards your energy." He rolled his eyes but played along.

He cut the cards once and handed me the deck, following my orders. I spread them out. First, his significator: the Ten of Swords, possibly the worst card of all, with a solitary, prostrate figure under a black sky, pierced in the back by all ten swords. It represents, in Waite's words, "pain, affliction, tears, sadness, desolation." The rest of the cards weren't much better. From the minor arcana, more swords. From the major arcana, he pulled the Tower, a card signaling corruption, destruction, and the presence of evil. He got the Death card, too. The Celtic Cross turned up little more than despair. And as much as I disliked the guy, I *really* didn't like what I saw in those cards. Not for anyone, not even for him.

I kept quiet for a few moments while I tried to figure out

how to spin this. Anyone who read tarot cards knew that the Death card was not to be taken literally. It did not forecast imminent peril. It was about transformation: dramatic but necessary change. And the Tower, menacing as it was, *might* signal the obliteration of the negative forces in his life. But that Ten of Swords? I couldn't get around it, especially since it was his significator. Had it landed upside down, that would've tempered its meaning and softened the blow. But as it was, right side up, full strength, there was nothing good I could say. Maintaining eye contact is key to being a good mystic, but I couldn't even meet his gaze.

"Well, what's it say?" he finally asked.

I took a deep breath. "None of this is carved in stone or written in blood—"

He cut me off. "Well. *What?*"

So I told him what I saw. Things looked bad. Where destruction was already underway, there was likely more to come. The isolation, aloneness, and despair he felt held out little hope of diminishing anytime soon. Change was coming, that was clear, and it would be something dramatic, but probably not for the better. And as I interpreted one dismal set of symbols after another, the guy leaned in closer, put his elbows on the table, buried his head in his hands, and started to cry.

He told me that his marriage was falling apart. That he constantly worried about his health. That he was too young for heart problems, but he had them anyway. That he felt as though his whole life had added up to zero. He asked: "Will I ever be happy?" The cards, I answered bluntly, said no.

"But," I told him, just like I told everyone else, "you have the power to change that." He shook his head and glared at me with red, swollen eyes that said *No. I don't.*

I did not want to believe him, but I held myself back. I had no business contradicting him, arguing with him, trying to make him feel hopeful. Maybe he was right. Maybe he didn't have the power. Maybe no one had the power. Maybe the days that lie ahead of us are set in stone and written in blood, and that was that. And it occurred to me that maybe I'd been the cynic: Something I had believed in had become a shtick, a gambit for attention. I hadn't thought it through. Maybe I'd even hurt people.

In the background, other passengers were caught up in conversation, laughing and drinking and carrying on. I could think of nothing more to say to the guy. Nothing reassuring. I felt small and foolish, incapable of any small comfort or kindness, and when the guy got off the train a couple of stops before mine, I was relieved.

I sat awake in my bed that night and thought about him. I imagined him going home to a white-clapboard colonial, to an unhappy wife pretending to be asleep. I imagined him returning the next day to a job he hated and getting wasted again that afternoon. But of course at fifteen, I really *couldn't* imagine what it was like to be him, to live his life. And I realized I didn't want to be able to. I didn't want to be adult enough yet to understand where he was coming from. Reading tarot cards in the bar car had been fun until it got serious. Adults had problems I could not begin to fathom, that I should not wish on myself, no matter how badly I wanted to grow up. And they had things to say I wasn't ready to hear, and to which I was incapable of responding with any real empathy.

I didn't go back to the bar car. I missed the drinks. I missed the grown-ups. I missed their attention. But I was *not* one of them. For the first time in my life—but not the last—I felt sharply and unhappily aware that I was getting older. That I wasn't exactly a child anymore. I was in the borderlands, neither here nor there, old enough to see that I was too young for the bar car, even though I desperately wanted to be there. I had been little more than a pretender, but I had felt, at least for a little while, like a regular, and for reasons I didn't yet understand, that feeling mattered to me, and I sensed that it always would. But I knew I didn't belong there—not yet—although I could feel adulthood encroaching, real adulthood, which now seemed less about drinking and smoking and freedom and more about loss and fear and the sense that Death itself lay waiting somewhere just ahead.

2.

TWENTY-ONE SHOTS

Inglewood and Santa Cruz

My mother just had to go to a show and see it first-hand, I figured, and everything would be fine. She'd see that the people were nice, and no one really got hurt, and she'd stop worrying so much about what I was up to. So during the Grateful Dead's nine-night run at Madison Square Garden in 1988, I hooked her up with a pair of tickets. She invited her friend Eva. Ma showed up at the Garden in a dress and Eva in tight, ironed dark jeans and a blazer. They both wore good jewelry, sunglasses, heels, and full makeup. Two cosmopolitan New York ladies, out on the town, taking in dinner and a concert. I pointed them in the direction of their seats and called out, "Have a good show," as they descended into the belly of the Garden. "Come back and hang out during intermission." A real Deadhead didn't go to her seat. I stayed in the hallway with my friends, where the sound was fine and there was more room to hang out and dance and, if the spirit moved you, spin yourself into a trance.

Not three songs into the first set, I heard the *click-click-click* of their high heels returning to the hallway. "Ma, what's wrong?" I asked. She raised her sunglasses, just a little. I could see she was crying, and she said, "I can't talk to you now. I can't talk to you now. I can't talk to you now." My mother understood the magic in saying a thing three times. "Eva and I are leaving," she announced, avoiding direct eye contact with me. "We are going to have a drink. Then I am going home." She took a rumbly tearful breath and continued. "And I will talk to *you* tomorrow."

Some skinny stringy-haired kid slumped on the floor against the wall had been sizing up the situation. He looked at Eva and asked, "Hey, do you have a Valium?" She opened up her purse, shook a few pills out of a vial, and handed them to the kid.

He was clearly a genius. I, on the other hand, was totally fucked. I knew I was in big trouble with my mom, even if I did not understand why. I slept outside the Garden that night, in a pile of hippie kids under a pile of blankets, taking swigs from a flask of Jack Daniel's and trying to figure out what had made my mother cry. As far as I knew, the concert had proceeded without incident: no random acts of violence, no mass nudity, no college kid on a bad trip being hauled out on a stretcher. But I was sure she must have had her reasons, and I also knew that, in time, they would be revealed to me.

When I finally went home the next day, I found out what

had upset Ma. We sat together in the living room and talked, and she was eerily calm. She didn't object to the odd joint now and again herself—she was no Puritan—but the sheer *quantity* of smoke at the show had freaked her out. I guess I'd just gotten used to it. Oh, and one other thing: the personal hygiene situation. Never before had she seen so many brazenly filthy people. "Do those people *ever* shower?" she asked, horrified. By then she'd seen me through a few bouts of plantar warts on my feet, but she didn't even know about the scabies outbreak during the previous spring's tour. Yet it is only in retrospect—twenty years on now—that I can finally 'fess up and say: Yes, yes, it is likely that in becoming a Deadhead, along with asserting my independence, forging my identity, following my bliss, blah blah blah blah blah, I was also deliberately torturing my mother (who wasn't easy to shock, so it took some doing). Back then I hadn't so much seen it that way. If nothing else, after her aborted evening at the Garden, my mother was sure I was smoking about a pound of pot weekly and not bathing a whole lot. The drugs and the dirty: this got to Ma. But, like many casual observers, what she didn't notice was that many of us were also drunk.

Soon after I turned sixteen, with the encouragement of an unusually progressive guidance counselor who'd seen more than a few Dead shows himself, I dropped out of high school. Would it matter? I had already cut classes. A lot of them. And in the classes to which I'd bothered showing up, I was frequently overtaken by daydreaming. Or writing poems. Or worrying about the contras and the Sandinistas, nuclear power, the British miners, the Ethiopian famine, the sinking of the *Rainbow Warrior,* and how Ronald Reagan was ruining the world.

I don't recall ever doing my homework. I felt like I was wasting my time and my teachers' time. My mother, to say the least, was not pleased with my decision to drop out, but she understood that I was unhappy, adrift, and desperate to do something else, and she consented. I promised I'd get my equivalency diploma someday. And go to college someday. For now, I wanted to hit the road. I wanted to see the U.S. of A. I wanted to *live it.* I didn't even have to learn how to drive—there was always some other Deadhead with room for one more, one more who could pitch in for gas, for tolls, for the odd motel room or campsite.

Most of the jobs available to a teenage high school dropout with a limited skill set were in retail and service. That suited me fine. A couple of months of working in a bookstore could furnish the modest capital required to launch a cottage industry in tie-dyed apparel, handmade beaded jewelry, or vegetarian chili—or maybe even to get a plane ticket to the Bay Area for a big event like the annual New Year's Eve show. I'd get a job near home, keep it for a season, then pile into someone's rusty VW bus or sputtering van—someone, some friend, some stranger, no matter—and spend the next six weeks or so on tour.

It played out like that for more than a year, and then even that was not enough. I wanted to leave, period. No more three months on, three months off. No more bookstores, no more New York, no more Ma. And so, after an autumn of selling art books in Soho, I packed it in and left, with no intention of returning. I parlayed my final paycheck into a flight to San Francisco, where, just across the bridge in Oakland, a few nights of Grateful Dead shows awaited. I was not traveling light. I took an Army-Navy duffel bag crammed full of clothes and books, my tarot cards, a portable typewriter, and about a hundred bucks in cash.

On the flight out west, I sat next to a middle-aged man in a suit. I had on a favorite getup: a woven purple-and-green Guatemalan shmatte (a thing not so different from a dyed burlap sack, really) and a pair of tattered huaraches. The guy told me he was an actuary. I had no idea what that could possibly mean. He tried to explain. Anyway, he was a nice guy. We talked. He was going to some kind of meeting, he said. "And you?"

"I'm going to see the Grateful Dead."

He smiled. "Oh, I saw them a couple times. Years ago. Back in college." And then he got that glassy-eyed sweet-sad look, and sighed that sigh I knew from the guys in the Metro-North bar car, that sigh that says *Nostalgia is a bitch, and getting old is hard.*

"Then what?" he asked.

Then what? I had no idea.

"I have no idea," I said. Beyond a few days at the Oakland Coliseum, whatever else my future held was a mystery.

"Well, I sure hope you're careful," he said. "I have a daughter almost your age. I'd be worried out of my mind." By then I'd managed to get him to shift a mini bottle of Jack Daniel's—which I liked to think of as my signature drink, in homage to Janis Joplin—my way. The irony was not lost on me. There was plenty to worry about. The world, the big unpredictable one that is away from home, trembles with dangers—big ugly ones right out there on the surface, and other, more insidious ones pulsing just below. And for girls, it is fair to say there are more, and greater, dangers.

As much as I wished to believe in the Grateful Dead tour as a peaceable and equitable kingdom, it was not, and it did not exist in a protected magical circle. On an earlier tour, somewhere in upstate New York, my friends and I picked up a dead-eyed girl named Colleen. She was a little older than us, late twenties maybe. She wound up sharing a motel room with us that night. She stayed in the shower for about forty minutes, and then sat speechless on the bed bundled in towels and blankets for a long time. Another girl and I sat beside her, our arms around her, while she sobbed. And then she told us, even though we'd already figured out the essentials of what had happened: Just a few days earlier, she'd been raped in a campground. There were plenty of other Deadheads around, but nobody came to her rescue. Nobody pressed charges. Nobody took her to the hospital. "Everyone was fucked up," she told us—like she had to apologize for them.

Although many people I befriended on tour shared my burgeoning commitment to progressive politics in a broad, vague way, the environment could hardly be called feminist. Gender lines, to my surprise and dismay, were strictly drawn. Girls were expected to wear long and flowing—that is, feminine—clothes, to be pretty in a kind of standardized long-haired, patchouli-scented way. Men were expected to drink harder, do drugs harder, and at the same time, effectively govern the community. In some sense, women—along with drugs and booze—were treated kind of like community property on tour, even as there were inevitably some who kept their stashes to themselves. It all seemed so hunter-gatherer to me, and it was reinforced, perhaps even encouraged, by some of the lyrics to some of our favorite songs: "We can share the women, we can share the wine," Jerry Garcia and Bob Weir harmonized on "Jack Straw." One of the band's great crowd-pleasers, "Sugar Magnolia," is nothing less than a paean to an idealized hippie chick, hypersexualized but otherwise utterly undemanding, a girl with no interesting thoughts of her own, yet who is capable of getting her man out of all manner of countercultural scrapes.

None of that was on my mind as I flew west that day,

drinking Jack Daniel's and talking to the actuary. All I knew—and this was enough—was that as soon as I got off the BART from SFO to the Oakland Coliseum, I would not be alone. My friends would be there: I would find Danny and Billy, a clever pair of pothead Jersey boys I'd first met at Madison Square Garden, in the same series of shows to which I'd made the mistake of inviting my mother. I'd find Marie, a college dropout who'd grown up on an Indian reservation in Wyoming, whom I'd met that summer at a show at Giants Stadium and who helped me hone my bead-working skills and riveted me with her true stories of the American West. Ben would probably be in Oakland, too, a sweet Canadian just on the brink of too much LSD consumption whom a former tour buddy of mine and I had picked up hitching on our way to a show in Atlanta (or Greensboro? Much of this time, many of these places, have blurred for the obvious reasons—time, youth, drugs, and drink). And Lee, another Canadian, one of the first boys I fell for, with long blond hair and messed-up teeth, hyper and troubled and extremely funny in an open, shameless way.

They were all there, waiting for me in the Coliseum parking lot like I'd counted on. My new family—a family composed, effectively, of children intent on being something other than children, if not quite adults. A family who, to my mother, when she ultimately met some of its members and saw pictures of others, looked like nothing so much as the

Manson family. But they—*we*—were not that, nothing like that, not even close. We were not in the business of killing movie stars. We didn't want to hurt anyone—except, in a distant and abstract kind of way, our own families. We were mostly decent if slightly wayward kids who, for a variety of reasons, needed to leave the people who had raised us and who, many of us felt, had failed to understand us, and make a family of our own. Many came from messed-up homes. Some were fleeing abusive parents. (I didn't have it nearly as bad as many of my friends did, but I was tired of arguments with my mother.) We drank and danced, bartered bootlegs, got high and hung out, lived in vans and slept in cars under piles of stripy Mexican blankets in need of a good washing; we gave one another scabies and sometimes worse, and sometimes money, and often pot, and really whatever we had, sold trinkets and tofu stew, and for the most part, though not always, looked after one another. We stretched our young legs at truck stops along interstates, and at "scenic outlooks" dotting the highways. We camped alfresco in woods and on beaches. "How many Deadheads does it take to screw in a lightbulb?" Lee asked me once. "NONE! Deadheads screw in sleeping bags!" We were young. We had left our homes. We loved one another.

Three shows in Oakland and then—then—came the bigger question. Where to next? "Come to Vancouver," Ben said. "I've got a place to live and good people. We'll find you a job. And it's beautiful there. *Really* beautiful. You'll love it." The potential promise of a place to live, and even a way to earn some money: That was option number one, and it sounded all right. The alternative was to catch a ride down the California coast with Danny and Billy in the former's wreck of an old Dodge van for three nights of Dead shows in Inglewood, just outside Los Angeles. Danny had made a shitload of tie-dyed shirts—let it not be said that we were a uniformly lazy lot; this kid didn't lack for work ethic—and could use some help shilling them, and I also had some beaded jewelry to sell. So I'd have a few days of work. And then, *who knew?* And who gave a rat's ass? Not me. Sure, Vancouver sounded sensible. But sensible wasn't what I was after, really. What I was after was more shows. More fun.

On the way to Los Angeles we camped one night at Half Moon Bay, a place sacred to us, a homing ground on the shore, pitching our tents as close to the water's edge as we could manage. There were maybe a half dozen of us, and we ate hummus sandwiches on chunky health-food-store bread that smelled like freshly mowed lawn, and we sat by the fire, quietly telling stories and laughing under a huge starry sky. And for the first but not the last time in my life on tour, I felt a sensation of freedom that nearly overcame me, as though I were having an out-of-body experience of the kind I'd read about during a brief and miserable stint selling Time-Life's *Mysteries of the Unknown* series over the phone from a

windowless midtown office bearing above the door the inspirational legend THROUGH THESE DOORS PASS THE GREATEST
TELEMARKETERS IN THE WORLD. (And also, I can report, one
of the all-time worst.) At Half Moon Bay, freedom was what
I felt, overwhelmingly—and also the thing that otherwise
unhappy teenagers might just need most, the feeling that
finally, *finally*, I had found my people, that they got me, that
until then I had been a changeling in a world for which I had
not been equipped, and now I was where I had always right-
fully belonged. I shared a small tent that night with Lee, not
doing much of anything—just talking, kissing, his breath
warm on my neck and face, reeking of Molson.

The next morning we bought vegetarian burritos and
headed south in a little convoy to LA, switching at some
point from the majestic Pacific Coast Highway to the unpic-
turesque 5 for the sake of time. We pulled into the Forum
parking lot, quickly scored tickets for all three shows, made a
killing on shirts and jewelry. Such a killing that it wouldn't
be necessary to sleep in the van, or in sleeping bags outside
the Forum. We could get a motel room where we could
shower and watch TV and drink beer and get high in peace
and privacy. We were feeling so flush that on the last night
of the Dead's Inglewood run, damn, we could even hit
the motel lounge—a divey, tiki-ish little shithole of a bar.
Perfect.

The culture, such as it was, of the Grateful Dead tour will

always be associated more closely with drugs—marijuana and psychedelics, by and large, for which I did not lack enthusiasm—than drinks. But there was *plenty* of drinking on tour, and by then I knew where my deepest allegiance lay. A segment of tourheads drank with greater gusto than the rest and owed, perhaps, a spiritual debt to Ron "Pigpen" McKernan, one of the band's founders, a blues-drenched keyboardist who succumbed to internal hemorrhaging resulting from his alcoholism in 1973 at age twenty-seven (like Janis, Jim, and Jimi), and who, it has been said, never shared his bandmates' devotion to LSD, preferring Thunderbird and Southern Comfort.

I loved a good acid trip as much as the next Deadhead. In high school, I'd pretty much spent every waking hour stoned off my ass. But now, as a full-time tourhead, I had new and daunting responsibilities. I had a business to run—selling shirts and jewelry and other homespun commodities, doing tarot card readings, and trolling for "miracles," the word in our lingua franca for free tickets. The sleaziest, most surefire method I knew for scoring miracles was to borrow a baby from a friend on tour who had a couple of them. If I set off in one direction with a baby strapped to my back and she took the other in another direction, the sorry spectacle of two sad-eyed teenage Deadhead moms could yield more tickets separately than one mom and two babies could.

And that was about as much tour math as I could manage. Mostly I was incapable of making transactions of any kind when I was stoned or tripping. I knew plenty of hippie hustlers who could exchange money, make change, do business on a few tabs of acid. I couldn't for the life of me figure out how they managed it. Hand me a ten-dollar bill when I was tripping and forget it: suddenly Alexander Hamilton was Neptune, rising from a roiling rainbow sea, floating forth unto the universe wielding his trident and making tulips grow from cracks in the sidewalk. And for that ten, if, say, I owed you five, chances were good that I'd blithely slip you a twenty, and instead of just acknowledging that I was too fucking high to make the right change, you might be all, "Hey, thanks, sister, right on," as though I'd intended all along to redistribute the wealth in some well-meaning hippie way.

In fact, I needed money badly, more than ever. And high, I was incapable of making any. So, improbable as it may seem, becoming a full-time tourhead put an abrupt, uncalculated end to my most dedicated phase of drug consumption. But a few beers—in this way the parking lot scenes outside of Dead shows were no different from those at football games or any other locus of collective effervescence, and always had beer entrepreneurs toting huge coolers and barking "Ice-cold imports!" from aisle to aisle—and I was just fine. A few swigs of Jack Daniel's from a hip flask? Hell, even better. And that weekend in LA, with my crocheted, rainbow-colored Guatemalan satchel bursting with cash, I could buy all the Jack Daniel's I'd ever wanted. Danny and Billy and I and a few other friends we'd said could crash in the motel

room with us hit the bar—with no idea that I was heading
for the single drunkest night of my life.

The next morning, December 11, 1989, I awakened on a
greasy, flattened stretch of carpet in that cheap motel
room in Inglewood with a nearly rigid disk of my own shit
stuck to my backside. I peeled it off in a single perfect pan-
cake and thought immediately of a film I'd seen a year or so
before in a high school social studies class—an elective
beloved of all the stoners called Indian and Southeast Asian
Studies. The film was about village life in India. I thought of
the thin, dark-haired women in faded saris setting cow dung
patties out in the sun to dry for cooking fuel.

The sunshine pushing through fissures in the dusty
drapes looked and felt like early morning light—diffuse and
uncertain. It was probably around six. I had been sleeping
under a desk, which the top of my head grazed as I sat up. I
glanced around and quickly calculated that more than a half-
dozen dirty hippies were crammed into every corner and
crevice of the room: a blond-dreadlocked guy on the floor in
front of the TV, three or four kids sprawled across the king-
size bed, someone laid out in the space between the bed and
the radiator, a girl in a diaphanous purple dress curled up in
a chair. I do not remember if I managed to get up, flush the
shit, and clean myself up, or if I just drifted back into sleep,
my head buzzing with images of emaciated cows and fields

of marigold. I do not remember much from the night before when, I was told later, I drank some twenty-one shots of Jack Daniel's. Marie, who had left the bar before things got ugly, was furious with Billy and Danny, who, she said, had encouraged my recklessness because they wanted to see exactly how much I was capable of drinking.

"I lost count," Billy said. Apparently we'd all gotten good and hammered, but I'd gone above and beyond. In *Inglewood*, for God's sake, which to New Yorkers is like saying you spent the drunkest night of your life in *Newark*.

"You kept going on about Irish mythology," Danny added. "Ranting about gods and goddesses."

I did?

Well, that was plausible. I'd been reading Yeats and Lady Gregory. And some moony New Age-y manifesto on the spirituality of the ancient Celts.

"It was pretty funny." By which I knew he meant I'd made a complete ass of myself.

Huh.

What I *do* remember is this, and only this: a lame bartrick parlor-game kind of thing, with which the waxymustachioed, Hawaiian-shirted barman in the motel lounge had dazzled and, I confess, stumped me. I still trot it out from time to time and, amazingly, it almost always trips people up—*especially* smart people, even after only one drink. For this you'll need a penny, a nickel, and a dime.

This can be quite dramatic. Hold on to the coins. Maybe

shake them up in your palm for a few seconds, then blow on them. First you say, deadpan, "Johnny's mother had three children." Then you slap the penny down on the bar with one decisive stroke of the thumb and announce, "The first one was Penny."

Next, lay the nickel down and say, a little more casually, "The second one was Nicholas."

Finally, slam down the dime, hard. And when you're good and ready, ask, with great intention, like you're interrogating a perp, *"Who was the third?"*

Nine out of ten times, the poor idiot will say Dimitri.

Anyway, I remember nothing else—at least, the mind's catalog of images and sound has gone dark and quiet. But my nose and my sense of taste recall more: To this day, even the smell of Jack Daniel's—tinged with burnt cotton and vanilla—makes me want to retch. And that is precisely what I spent the earliest morning hours of December 11 doing, attended to by Marie. After the boys hoisted me up the stairs from the bar, I heard later, she held my head over the toilet, splashed water on my face and implored me to drink as much of it as I could, and watched over me to make sure I didn't die. On a few occasions, I've thought back on this and worked myself close to anger. Shouldn't someone have taken me to the hospital? Couldn't I have died? Well, yes. But I am never quite able to get angry. Partly because we were all young and had little idea what to do in such a situation. Partly because so much of the romance of tour life resided in its near-lawlessness, in its frontier-outlaw contempt and near-obsessive avoidance of authority, of The Man. Partly, I am also sure, because there were times back then when *I* certainly should have done something and didn't, and I want to excuse myself, too. On tour, we made excuses for ourselves, and for one another, a lot.

I fell back asleep under the desk. The next time I woke up, I was some three hundred and fifty miles north of Inglewood, in Santa Cruz, aware that I was lucky to be alive, lucky to have had people looking after me, even if we were all too young to know how to take care of anyone, ourselves included. I considered kissing the ground, the dark dusty asphalt of a strip-mall parking lot near Domino's Pizza, near Baskin-Robbins, near the Saturn Café—a legendary vegetarian joint with a solidly vegan-feminist clientele at the time. My head was heavy, pulsing at the temples and the back. At sunset we went to the beach, the sweet state beach with its natural bridges of enormous eroded rocks. We lit up a joint and watched the surfers, the students, the drifters who'd long preceded our own drifting to this place, who had probably arrived here much as we did, only years before, with no better plan, traveling the same tine in the same forked road: Santa Cruz or Vancouver, Santa Cruz or San Francisco, Santa Cruz or Humboldt, Santa Cruz or _____, Santa Cruz or _____, Santa Cruz or _____. Santa Cruz instead of anywhere else, especially instead of wherever they'd come from.

Danny and Billy and I lived in that van, parked on

Mission Street, in front of the pizzeria where they worked, at least through Christmas, at which time Danny had managed to scrounge together enough money to return to New Jersey for the holidays. Billy was a Christian, but not a religious one. Still, Christmas was Christmas. And I was one of those half-assed New York Jews who grew up celebrating Easter *and* Passover—whose family, truth be told, preferred Christmas to Hanukkah, because Ma really loved chestnuts roasting on an open fire, and overstuffed stockings, and a nice Bûche de Noël and all that, without particularly paying Jesus any mind, though she was firmly of the opinion that he seemed like a totally okay guy. So even for me, yes, Christmas *was* Christmas, and sleeping in a van would not do, nor would eating discards from the pizzeria.

"We should at least get a room somewhere," I suggested. "Sleeping in the van on Christmas just seems wrong." Billy quickly agreed, even though we were both close to broke. We checked in to the cheapest motel we could find. At a convenience store across the road, for a small fee, we got a loitering grown-up to procure a few six-packs of Anchor Steam for us—the birth of the baby Jesus rated at least a classy regional beer.

"Should we get some Jack, too?" Billy asked, half-serious.

"Nah." No fucking way.

We settled into our motel room with our beer and our Cool Ranch Doritos and those cheese crackers with peanut

butter that cost a dollar for six packets—on account of welcoming the occasional junk food splash-out with great enthusiasm and, above all, on account of *Christmas*, we could
dispense with our usual hippie health-food-store totally organic food pieties—and flipped on the TV, each of us claim-
ing our own queen-size bed. Billy and I were friends, but not
especially close friends, and without Danny we had little to
say to each other. We idly watched the local news, then some
cartoons, then some videos on MTV. When the clicker
landed on the Yule log, we gave each other a look of faint
despair. This was our Christmas, our sad, weird Christmas,
and a motel room was nearly as shitty a place to be as the van.
Doritos and beer were good, but shouldn't we go out for
dinner?

"Shouldn't we go out for dinner?" I asked.

No argument from Billy. "Let's do it."

We hit the strip—the pedestrian mall in downtown Santa
Cruz—and checked the menus posted outside the restaurants. Every place was either too expensive or full, or both,
or closed. We trudged up to Mission Street. The vegetarian
café was open. Of course it was open, but it did not *do* Christmas. No twinkling lights. No tinsel. No Santas or reindeer or
candy canes. But there were free tables, and it was better
than our stash back at the motel. We ordered salads and
lentil soup, and the conversation stayed sparse. I kept my
thoughts to myself: I wished I were at home, not for good,

just at that moment. I missed my family, imperfect as we were. I envied Danny, who at this moment was probably reneging on his vegetarianism and eating ham or turkey in the company of his relations, young and old; who was probably luxuriating in the flickering light of a Christmas tree; who was in the Northeast, where there was likely snow on the ground and maybe even children sledding, where Christmas was Christmassy, not like this warm West Coast horseshit. I envied Danny, who was having a *real* Christmas, so different from Billy's and mine, surrounded as we were by recalcitrant atheists picking at tofu and brown rice. What was I doing here? Why had I chosen *this*? And I imagined that Billy, my reticent, accidental Christmas companion, was thinking much the same.

We walked quickly back to the motel in the cooling California night, past palm trees and strip malls, past so many parked cars and so few people. I glanced into the homes of strangers, through casement windows framing repeated tableaux of families being families at Christmastime, families drinking egg nog and, I imagined, listening to Bing Crosby crooning "The Christmas Song" and Ella Fitzgerald elevating "Jingle Bells," wishing one and all—except for me, except for Billy—a swinging Christmas, as they tallied their holiday hauls. We returned to our motel room, to our matching queen-size beds, to our already diminished six-packs. We drank silently, a few feet apart, isolated by our unhappiness.

I do not remember if Billy called home, but I know I did not. I had elected this estrangement and would ride it out. We resumed our channel-flipping. Fuck the news and its cheerful reports of Christmas near-miracles and charitable acts. Fuck the Yule log and all its stupid Yule logness.

"Hey Billy, pass me another Anchor Steam."

"You got it."

And there we were. Two depressed teenagers far from home, far from parents and brothers and sisters, with no presents, no tree, no stockings, no cards, no calls, no high school diplomas, no home save a crappy brown van, pounding back bottles of beer, lying on dingy, quilted, motel bedspreads, tired but restless.

Flick. On the next channel: *The Sound of Music*. Beautiful pixie-haired Julie Andrews, Sister Maria—not yet betrothed to the Captain, not yet a von Trapp—comforting her little Austrian charges with a litany of her favorite things. *Doorbells and sleigh bells and schnitzel with noodles!* And I thought of Ma back in New York and her inexhaustible cheerleading for The Great American Musical, her love of all things Rodgers and Hammerstein, Lerner and Loewe, Irving Berlin, Jerome Kern and George Gershwin and Lorenz Hart. I thought of Sunday evenings when I was even younger, in my grandfather's little library, listening to the original cast recording of every cast that had ever originally been recorded. And I could see something stirring in Billy, too, something possibly warm and good, though I was certain that in his case it had nothing to do with show tunes, and I watched as the fear and fretfulness slowly, slowly started to wash away from his young, unshaven face. And I noticed, for the first time, what a fine face he had: both strong and soft, high cheekbones and Elvis-y lips and pretty blue eyes. Was he thinking of his favorite things? Well, God only knew what those were in Billy's case—but suddenly, damn it if we *didn't* feel so bad, if we felt, actually, pretty okay. And damn if by the time "Edelweiss" rolled around, small and white and blooming and growing forever, I wasn't singing along with the brave, elegant (and, let us be honest, pretty fucking hot) Captain von Trapp strumming his guitar. And that feeling of freedom returned, that sense that even if I didn't know what I was doing, what I was doing was fine, then and there, was right. We both cried; it was good. In my case, the tears flowed free and fast. Billy was more restrained, but a few droplets stained his cheeks, even though he was trying to fight them.

"Hey Billy?"

"Yeah?"

"Pass me another beer."

"You got it."

"Thanks. Hey Billy?"

"Yeah?"

"Merry Christmas, man."

He turned his eyes away from the television, looked at me, and nodded. "Yeah, Merry Christmas."

A week later, the boys and I drove up to Oakland for the big New Year's show, where Vancouver Ben pressed a miracle ticket into my ready and grateful palm, where I spun around the broad corridors of the Coliseum with people I loved, where the night shifted itself down into dawn, into a new decade, into the 1990s. Then back to Santa Cruz, where Danny and Billy and I, joined later by Marie, found a place to live up in the hills, in a century-old log house on stilts right on top of a fault line in a forest of scrub oak and redwoods, Pacific madrones and ancient ferns and pillowy green moss.

I'm not a Deadhead anymore, and haven't been one in years. And there are some people who seem to regard that part of my life as a lapse in taste, a failure of discernment. That's okay by me; I don't regret it a bit. And I can't think about this without starting to cry a little, like I did in that motel room that Christmas night, because I look back at my sixteen-, seventeen-year-old self, in some carnival of a parking lot somewhere in America, with no class to go to, no job to worry about, no parents on my case, with the certainty that some-how, through luck and providence and the kindness of strangers, there would be food enough when I was hungry, a place to crash when night came, someone to drink with or to hold fast to when I was lonely, and I get this pain, this pang, this awful, hopeless, close to desperate longing. I think I'd do anything if I could just go back there for one day, just one day. That's all I'd need. I don't think I'd want more. Nostalgia really is a bitch, and getting older is hard.

I grew up. And on the whole, I guess I'm glad I did. I left Santa Cruz. I got a GED. I went to college. Went to work. Got married. Moved on. Found other communities where I fit in, with other people I loved.

But I know that part of me will always long for that time, with its many joys and excesses and occasional terrors. I learned what it meant to go too far, to drink too much. And I had acquired something that would serve me immeasurably later on, when I fell in love with bars: I had become wide open to people, more capable of accepting them, and of enjoying them, and of loving them, for all their goodness, and badness, and general *mishegoss*. I grew bolder: I would talk to anyone, anytime. It almost always paid off; if not in friendship, at least in stories. I look back and what I see first are not tie-dyes and discarded nitrous oxide cartridges and ticket stubs and spiny green pot plants in lividly illuminated crawl spaces; what I see first are golden-white quivering aspens in autumn on the road from Flagstaff to the Grand Canyon. Sunset at Natural Bridges. I see a campfire in a backyard in suburban Rochester, where a very nice man named John Milton—for real—whose address had been given to us mysteriously by a bunch of bikers he didn't know, let a host of hippies unroll our sleeping bags in his living room, built a campfire for us in his backyard, and made us eggs and home fries and toast the next morning. Mostly, I see those people, and I hear the songs we sang together. I never felt freer in my life than I did in one of those parking lots, or around one of those campfires with those sweet unwashed people, and I'm telling you, brothers and sisters, I never will feel that free again.

3.

AN AMERICAN DRINKER
IN DUBLIN

Grogan's Castle Lounge, Dublin

I t is hard to say exactly when I became Irish. It's not like it happened all of a sudden. It was gradual, incremental. And the Irishness I was interested in had nothing to do with the Kennedys, the Catholic Church, the Clancy Brothers, the green-beer-and-kiss-me-I'm-Irish swag of Saint Patrick's Day in America. What I was after was an equally bogus and utterly ahistorical idea of an ancient Irishness that reflected, and galvanized, my vague, young, softheaded notions about poetry, revolution, and identity, and the romantic allure of islands, the way they are set apart from the rest of the world, isolated, troubled, special. My instinctive attraction to tribalism in many forms—from the fraternity of drinkers on the Metro-North bar car to the family of lost children I'd joined on the Grateful Dead tour—had found in the ancient Celts and their contemporary descendants yet another expression. Here was another tribe to which I wanted to belong.

For a Jewish girl from New York it was a questionable

choice—why on earth would I trade my inherent identifica-
tion with one historically oppressed people for another?—
and a peculiar feat of self-reinvention. Yeats's poems had a lot
to do with it. The Pogues had something to do with it. And
fairy tales, and myths, and legends. I was stirred by the stories of Hibernian badasses, from Cuchulainn to Brendan
Behan. I was a total sucker for the stolid somber pulse—like
heavy steady raindrops—of the bodhran, the big, round,
moonlike frame drum that is the dark heart beating within
spooky old ballads in which maidens were drowned in rivers
by jealous sisters, or babies were abducted by malevolent
elves, or plans were hatched to lead bloody midnight insur-
rections against colonial oppressors.

I had a sense that I would very much like the smell
of burning peat in a small parlor on a damp evening, and
like even better long leisurely afternoons in a pub on some
Dublin backstreet, where gray northern light asserted itself through mist-streaked, half-curtained windows, where I
might settle in with a pint of Guinness and a notebook, tin-
kering with my poems and maybe recording bits of overheard
conversations, while regulars argued politics and poetry and
talked and drank, talked and drank, talked and drank, until
at last a white-haired barman with rolled-up shirtsleeves
finally threw his arms up and shouted an exasperated "Last
call." I was sure not only that I'd fit in just fine, but that I
could keep up with them all—if not drink them right under
the table.

This is a landscape mined with cultural stereotypes, flattering ones and ugly ones, stereotypes all the same, and it is dangerous territory. Perhaps you have heard that we Jews love money and school. You may have also heard that we Jews don't drink. "No one has ever seen a Jewish drunk," my mother used to tell me.

Right.

You may have also heard that the Irish *do* drink, and prodigiously. So, for this and other reasons, by the time I entered college I had become Irish. And though I didn't stay Irish for long, I was pretty good at it. Second semester, I took an Irish literature survey class. I paced around campus reciting "The Stolen Child" and "The Second Coming" to anyone who would listen. James Connolly, the courageous and unabashed Socialist among the leaders of the Easter Rising, had joined Leon Trotsky and Antonio Gramsci in my little pantheon of radical gods. I learned a smattering of Irish Gaelic. I bought a bodhran.

It was hard to explain myself, though, and I was frequently interrogated. My heart was definitely in it; I loved, and knew, Irish folktales, and traditional music, and poetry. But why was I so into this? I didn't really know. Was it because my upbringing had been so secular, so open, so fertile for self-expression? Maybe, but I hardly thought about it that way. Really, I couldn't come up with an explanation better than "because it's interesting." It was true—Irish history and literature *are* interesting, but wasn't that also true

of Turkish or Russian or Japanese or—heaven help me—
English history and literature? I was deeply unsatisfied by my
lame answer to an honest question, maybe even exasperated.
I had dyed my hair red. I could easily pass. I was asked so
many times if I was Irish that after a point I decided to say
that, yes, yes I was, sort of.

My mother had often told me colorful stories about her
paternal grandmother, Anna. She had lived in Flat-
bush, Brooklyn, in a mixed neighborhood of aspirational
middle-class Eastern European Jews and Irish Catholics
whose children fought one another viciously as soon as the
parochial and public schools sprang them at the end of every
weekday afternoon. Anna sang and played piano, was famously foulmouthed, had left her Hungarian-Jewish husband, my great-grandfather—by all accounts a decent and
mild-mannered stationer—and, after the divorce, bore a second child, out of wedlock. She said "burl" for *boil* and "earl"
for *oil*. She was tough. She had cred. "You'd have thought she
was Irish," my mother, herself a great fan of the whole green-
beer-and-kiss-me-I'm-Irish Saint Patrick's Day thing, said approvingly. And so it was that my great-grandmother Anna,
whom I had never met, who was, conveniently, long dead,
became Irish. Once I'd decided that, when people asked,
"Are you Irish?" I would sheepishly answer, "Oh, *not really*.
Just one great-grandmother." It was a total crock, and I felt

slightly sick to my stomach whenever I repeated it.
it anyway, because it made me feel just a little less like ~~~
kind of poseur Irish manqué. Which of course was exactly
what I was.

In a hallway near the English department office at my
school, I saw a poster for a summer course in Irish studies at
Trinity College in Dublin. For months before I left that June,
it was all I could think about and talk about. I just couldn't
wait to get to Dublin, where I would read good books, find
the best pub in the world, and, I had it in my head, maybe
meet a real live Irish poet, who would have a lovely soft
accent and recite poems to me, and with whom, I hoped, I
might have a brief but memorable affair.

The kids in the summer program were told to meet at a
designated spot at Kennedy Airport, near the Aer Lingus
check-in area. I spotted them right away. They were clean-cut
and preppy in their khaki shorts and polos and fleece pull-
overs, well-adjusted and healthy-looking. I was not, in my
black leggings and Converse high-tops and nose ring, a pack
of Camel Lights distending the top left pocket of my denim
jacket, the dark rings under my eyes evidence of the hangover that had resulted from my send-off at a bar in the East
Village the night before. They gathered together in an excited
little circle. I did not join them. Instead, I sat by myself in one
of those contoured bench seats in a corner of the terminal,
drinking coffee and reading a translation of the ancient Irish
epic the *Táin*. And then I saw a guy walk in wearing a leather

jacket, its blackness brightened by an ACT UP button: a pink triangle on a black field, *Silence = Death*. Rad. We gave each other a look. I felt a little better.

On the flight I sat next to an Irish couple returning from a New York vacation. "First trip to Ireland?" the missus asked.

"Yes," I answered. "I'm going to study there for the summer."

"Oh, and where's that?"

"Dublin. Trinity College," I said.

"Top school," the mister said.

"Grand," the missus agreed.

They were done talking to me.

The in-flight movie was *The Field*. In it, the great Richard Harris (a film—and drinking—hero of mine, second only to Peter O'Toole) plays a pathologically bitter Irish tenant farmer who fears, not without justification, that he will be forced off his precious green field—which, the viewer is frequently reminded, he had nurtured and coaxed and agonized over and transformed by the sweat of his brow from a patch of hard rock into a lush and fertile pasture—by a rich Irish-American outsider. This does not go well. It ends with the deranged farmer driving his herd of cows off a cliff, into the roiling Atlantic, and unintentionally killing his dim-witted, sometimes violent son along with them.

It is not a film that makes Ireland look good. It depicts the Irish as insular, provincial, suspicious, incapable of adjusting to a changing world, and frankly insane. *This* was where I was dying to go to study? *These* were the people in whose history and culture I had so deeply immersed myself? I took a long look at the couple seated next to me. Maybe I'd made a serious mistake.

We arrived in Dublin in the early afternoon and were shepherded to our dorm at Trinity. I'd be sharing a two-bedroom suite with a pretty, blond, sweet-natured California girl whom I strongly suspected was still a virgin. She wore long white nightgowns and a retainer. She seemed scared of me. Like I might hit her, or hit on her.

After a quick nap I walked back through the college gates to check out the city. Dull, familiar chain stores flanked both sides of Grafton Street. I was upset by the spectacle of dozens of children—young children, under ten—begging on the pavement, mostly in boy-girl pairs, members of the Travelers community, I was told later that summer. One little girl in one such pair looked up at me with cold blue eyes. "Spare some change, miss?"

I didn't have any change yet. I offered to buy them something to eat; they didn't take me up on it. I was planning to minor in anthropology; I figured I should try to engage these unfortunates. "I promise I'll come back when I have change," I said, crouching to meet them at eye level. "What are your names?"

"Mary and John," the girl answered glumly.

I soon learned that, at least in the summer of 1991, all the beggar children of Dublin said their names were Mary and John.

So far, Dublin kind of sucked. Disappointed, I headed back to the dorm. A group of American girls was chattering in the stairwell, looking over the orientation program and class schedule. They were not enthusiastic about having to read poetry. Then what were they doing here? I wondered. But I kept my mouth shut.

Later in the evening I noticed the *Silence = Death* guy heading out of the suite next to mine. I tagged along. "I was so relieved when I saw you at the airport," I told him.

"I thought you looked nuts," he said.

His name was Ryan. He knew Dublin a little. His father was from Sligo, in the northwest of the Republic, and he had visited Ireland before with his family. He was a junior at the University of Chicago, studying music. We went to a packed nightclub not far from campus. I would've preferred a pub, but this would do. Ryan drifted away toward a cute boy. Another one drifted toward me, a little older, late twenties, and edged in next to me at the bar. "I'm Larry," he said, introducing himself. That didn't seem right. He seemed too young to be a Larry, and he worked in business in some vague way. But he was friendly and funny enough, and he paid for my pints and gave me pointers about his native city. He didn't seem particularly interested in poetry or politics or cultural identity, in anything that had drawn me to Ireland. It was hardly a conversation for the ages, but it improved with every emptied pint glass. By the end of the night I had drained at least five. Never mind the Book of Kells, Kilmainham Gaol, the GPO, Sandymount Strand: "What you really need to do here in Dublin," Larry opined, "is go to a rugby match." I was drunk enough to agree.

By then, Ryan had disappeared. Larry offered to walk me back to Trinity. At the college gate, he kissed me undramatically and said he'd pick me up there the following Saturday afternoon. Well, why not? Romantically, my freshman year back in Vermont had been a bust. I was game.

I soon learned that a rumor was rampant in Dublin: American girls were easy.

Larry showed up as scheduled on Saturday, and we walked and talked and eventually wound up at the Stag's Head, a venerable old pub with a long marble bar and lots of weathered wood. The Guinness was good. We were having a fine time. And then—and I can't for the life of me remember what precipitated this—he announced that he didn't like Jews.

"Oh really?"

"Really," he confirmed, adding decisively, "I just don't like 'em."

I knew that Dublin's Jewish population had dwindled down to next to nothing by the end of the twentieth century. After the Second World War, many Irish Jews emigrated to America and Israel. I knew about Robert and Ben Briscoe, the Jewish father and son who had both served as Lord High Mayors of Dublin. I knew about Portobello, the small Southside district once known as Little Jerusalem, where long ago James Connolly savvily distributed election pamphlets translated into Yiddish. I knew about the synagogue there, and about the small old bakery that sold something resembling a bagel; both still stood but were relics of former times. Larry could not have had significant opportunities to find himself in the company of Jewish people.

"Have you ever met one?" I asked, knowing by then that Larry hadn't traveled much out of Ireland.

"No, I can't say that I have." He gestured to the barman for another round.

"Well, now you have." That was the last thing I said to Larry. I left behind a full pint of Guinness. I had managed to assimilate so easily in Dublin that it was assumed I was Irish-American. But never had I felt more like a Jew, or more thrilled to be one.

Back at the dorm I ran into Ryan and told him what had happened. "Asshole," he agreed. "Forget about it. Anyway, I found a pub I *know* you'll like."

Ryan led me to South William Street, not far from Grafton. From the outside, Grogan's Castle Lounge wasn't especially promising or picturesque. But as soon as we entered, I knew I had found the bar that I had dreamed about in the months before my arrival in Dublin, and possibly my spiritual home. Aesthetically, it wasn't much: the carpets were tatty, the walls were covered with questionably competent paintings by local artists, the upholstery on the banquettes and barstools was a little dingy. But it was smoky and cozy and welcoming, and buoyant with conversation. In the '70s, a former barman from McDaid's—a well-known literary haunt—started working at Grogan's, and many of his writerly regulars followed him there.

I took a seat while Ryan went up to the bar to order our pints, and I pulled out a notebook and pen. A man two tables away called out to me, "Are you a writer, then?"

This is the first question they ask you at Grogan's. I was twenty. Was I a writer? How was I supposed to know?

"Yes," I answered.

"That's good," he said. "We're all writers here at Grogan's."

And that turned out to be pretty close to the truth. That night we met Peter, a handsome rake with jet-black hair and high cheekbones. In his bright yellow corduroys and pointy black leather shoes, he looked like a Mod filtered through

David Lynch movies. Peter didn't hesitate before taking out a crumpled sheaf of poems for me to peruse right there on the spot. With him was his sharp-tongued girlfriend, Kate—a student at Trinity—and their friend Michael, funny, awkward, self-deprecating, sweet, on the dole, in baggy sweatpants, a too-big T-shirt, and running shoes. He wrote, too, of course, but exactly what he wrote was anyone's guess. It was probably good, though. I sensed that he was the smartest of the bunch.

The lot of us shared a table, and for the first of many nights that summer I tossed my duty-free Camels and they their Marlboros and Silk Cuts on the table for all to share, and we bought round after round in turn, and laughed, and talked feverishly about the books we loved. Peter seemed to find my interest in his country's canon quaint and misguided.

"Whatever you do, for God's sake, just don't sing in here," Michael warned me in a grave whisper. He nodded in the direction of the genial, avuncular publican who looked like an Irish Santa Claus. "He once killed a man for singing in a pub." I believed him. I didn't find out until weeks later— when I repeated the story to someone else—that Michael had just been bullshitting me, taking the piss, as they say. Good one.

That first intoxicating night at Grogan's yielded three major developments. First, I was indoctrinated into the great Irish cultural tradition known as *craic* (pronounced *crack*— which disturbed me the first time I heard people talking about it, since New York was at the time in the thick of its devastating crack epidemic). *Craíc*, alongside Guinness, is major currency in a Dublin pub. It is discourse, conversation, chatter. It can be light or heavy, funny or serious. It can be about absolutely *anything*, but it must flow freely, it must have rhythm, and it must not be dominated by a single participant. There is good *craíc* and there is bad *craíc*. Grogan's was always good *craíc*.

Second, with alarming speed I acquired a taste for Irish whiskey, preferably Jameson. After my early romance with Jack Daniel's had come to its ugly end in California, I could no longer stomach even the smell of American whiskey, its redolent, deceptive sweetness. But Irish whiskey was a different thing altogether. Gentler, milder, less aggressively sugary. I still liked a pint of stout, but in Jameson I knew I had found my one true love. (I still defend Irish whiskey against frequent allegations that it is inferior to its Scottish counterparts, particularly to status-symbol single malts, and refer to spirits authority David Embury, who wrote, "If you really like the peat-smoke taste of Scotch, you may prefer it to Irish, just as you may prefer smoked ham to fresh ham. From every other point of view, however, I believe that Irish is infinitely superior to Scotch.")

Third, I discovered that the word *cunt*—totally forbidden where I came from, the worst of the worst, unholiest of unholies—could, if delivered with the right inflection, be light, affectionate, friendly, practically a term of endearment.

This took some getting used to, but by summer's end, I could unhesitatingly call my Irish friends complete fucking cunts and mean it in the nicest possible way.

Another night at Grogan's, not long after the first, a middle-aged man turned up at our usual table. All the regulars knew him and behaved differently in his midst. They sat up a little straighter and seemed to measure their words more carefully. Peter whispered his name in my ear. "Good poet," he said. "Published. A few books."

"So, you're a poet?" I asked him. By then, I knew how to start a conversation in Grogan's.

"I am," he said. And with that, we got to talking. And we kept talking. The Poet grew up in a small town, but had lived in Dublin since his twenties. He wore an unmistakable cloak of personal tragedy, which I found extremely appealing. He was exactly twice my age. And he was kind and attentive and laughed at my jokes and made meaningful eye contact. He had a beautiful, soft voice. He would read poems to me, I was sure, if I asked. Maybe I wouldn't even have to ask.

It was getting close to last call. "Michael and I are going to go to the workshop at the Oak this week," Peter told me. "You should come. Wednesday night."

"I'll be there," I promised.

"Bring a poem," he said.

On Wednesday evening I made my way to the basement of the Oak Bar on Dame Street. There must've been at least twenty poets there, sitting on folding chairs in a circle. They were young and old, talented and not, male and female—but mostly male. There were Angry Young Men and misty-eyed septuagenarians. Down-and-outers and chicly outfitted women of a certain age. I took a seat next to Peter and Michael. Michael nudged my shoulder and said, almost conspiratorially, "Look who's here." Across the room, I saw The Poet.

"Do you know why he came?" Peter asked.

"To read a poem, I would guess."

Peter arched a dark eyebrow. "He doesn't need *this*. He's here because he knew you'd be here."

I rolled my eyes and pretended I didn't care.

We went around the circle, and each participant read his or her poem aloud twice—or passed on reading that night and opted just to listen. Then, after each piece had been read, we went around the circle once more and everyone offered a brief critique, or passed. (At a meeting later in the summer, I saw a brawl break out in the workshop after an exceptionally stinging critique—something unknown to me from polite American poetry classrooms, and thrilling. And I'd heard about the time a courtly old codger, about to deliver his assessment of a piece by a self-styled tough guy, steeled himself to say, "Oh, it's a lovely poem, a lovely poem." He collected himself and looked away. "But mightn't it be better without the line *She could sit on my face any day*?" It had pained him to utter such words).

It was my turn. I don't remember what I read, likely something a little formal and stiff, faintly political and painfully earnest. The critiques were bland and nonabrasive. I could tell they were cutting the newcomer, the foreigner, some slack. Across the room, The Poet nodded his approval. I felt good. I'd survived my first round at the workshop.

Drinks upstairs followed. I sat with The Poet. He was a great talker, a vivid storyteller. He told me about his boyhood, about his years drifting around Europe teaching English. He had traveled. He had met Jews; he had no problem with that; he had even lived briefly in Israel, which was more than I could say for myself. Peter and Michael whispered to each other, smirking. *Fuck them,* I thought. We talked until last call, and The Poet walked me to Trinity.

"Can I kiss you?" he asked at the gate.

It was much better than my last kiss, with Larry the Jewhater. We said good night. The college gate was locked. I knocked loudly and the guards let me in. They liked to trap tipsy students in conversations from which it was diabolically difficult to extract oneself. Full-service security guards, one even insisted that I try *poitín*—coarse, fiery potato moonshine—while I was in Ireland. The other tried to teach me a few tin whistle tunes, but I was hopeless.

Within a week or so I had practically moved in with The Poet. He had a small house on the north side of the River Liffey, across the pedestrian Ha'penny Bridge. There was much that I found impressively self-sufficient about him, about his domesticity, this grown-up man in his little row house, who rose early every morning to bake bread and make a pot of strong black tea. And together we'd have our tea and toast before I headed out to Trinity for class, before he settled into his study for a full workday of writing. I admired his discipline.

By effectively moving out of the dorm—I still dropped by between classes, to grab a change of clothes, to take a nap or a shower, the odd night here and there—and in with an older man I had only just met, I had, Ryan told me, become a bit of a scandal. I received this news with great satisfaction. But in truth, nothing felt scandalous about my life with The Poet. More than anything else, we talked.

And we drank. Many evenings, after my classes had ended and he was satisfied with a day's writing, we'd meet at Grogan's. At the pub, he often drank shandies—concoctions of lager and 7UP far more popular among women than men. I'd usually stick to Guinness, holding off on whiskey until later, when we got home and would continue drinking and talking before dragging ourselves upstairs to bed. We were comfortable together. I felt secure. The Poet was affectionate and generous. He introduced me to old friends, to other writers. But we were not inseparable. I took nights off from The Poet—and even from Grogan's—to hang out with another group of friends I'd made at a rally, young radicals from the Socialist Workers Party, at *their* pub near the Bank of Ireland Plaza. The restrooms were tagged with scathing anti-English and anti-American graffiti. No one there asked if you were a writer. They didn't care, and—though they themselves were mostly students—they would have been much more impressed if you were a dockworker. No matter. If you knew the words to "The International," could hold your own in a discussion of Gramscian ideology (for a start, use the word *hegemony* as much as possible), *and* hold your liquor, you were in.

Trinity College had dropped down to the bottom of my list of Dublin priorities. I went to my classes. I took my exams. I stared at the clock until I could bolt out of the lecture hall and over to Grogan's. Most—though not all—of the teachers operated under the assumption that Americans were idiots, and accordingly dumbed everything down for us. To be fair, many of the Americans in Dublin, traveling in packs and vomiting in the streets, did little to disabuse anyone of this notion, and were outdone only by the Australians. One instructor, an ingratiating poet of some renown, told us that he thought Jim Morrison was a great poet. I knew this to be untrue and found it patronizing.

But I did get an education. At Grogan's. At the young

socialists' bar. From Ryan (who introduced me to my favorite pub *and* to Baudelaire's *Paris Spleen*) and from The Poet. I had made smart, interesting friends. I had found my pub. I was intimately involved with a real poet. I hated thinking that I'd have to leave, and soon.

"Just stay," Michael pleaded. "We'll find a way to get you on the dole." It was tempting. I was very happy in dear dirty Dublin.

A nother night, later in the summer. Another long, raucous shift at Grogan's, with Ryan and his boyfriend Eamonn, Peter and Kate, Michael, The Poet, and me. The *craic* was more cracking than usual. But when the barman shouted "last call," we drank up and then went our separate ways—Ryan and Eamonn to an after-hours gay club, Peter and Kate to their place, Michael, God knows where. The Poet and I walked home past the packs of Americans and Australians still stumbling around Dame Street and Temple Bar, past several pairs of begging John-and-Marys, along the Southside quays, across the Ha'penny Bridge. Once in a while we'd stop and kiss against a lamppost. We said little.

Back home he set a half-full bottle of Paddy on the table. We finished it off and went upstairs. He held me and kissed my back. And then he said, "There's something I have to tell you."

I turned to face him.

"I love you," he continued. "But there's someone else I'll always love more."

You've got to be fucking kidding me, I thought, as if he had said something singularly audacious and impertinent—and hurtful. I thought that I was in charge of this relationship, if only by virtue of my youth. I was mistaken.

The Poet went on, told me more. I quietly fumed and said nothing. I pulled on some clothes and collected the stuff I'd been keeping at his place—underwear and T-shirts and socks and a toothbrush, a few books—and crammed it into my backpack. I'd go back to the dorm. Immediately. I had started to cry. I announced that I was leaving.

"You don't have to do that," he said.

By then it was raining. I had no umbrella. I stomped unafraid past the drunken toughs who congregated at the next corner. I was seething, and still crying. With every block, the rain fell harder. By the time I reached the bridge, my clothes were soaked through and water had collected in my backpack. I was sorry to see that a few John-and-Marys were still out, so late, in the pouring rain. Even they seemed to take pity on me. "Ah, you'll be all right, miss," one boy said. "Spare some change?"

I dug some coins out of a pocket and pressed them into his small, cold palm. And I stood there, smack in the middle of the Ha'penny Bridge, listening to the rain hit the river, looking at this dirty old city I'd grown, in so little time, to love so fiercely, to feel at home in. I suddenly felt like this wasn't real, like I had suddenly become aware of how absurd this situation was, how absurd *I* was.

By then, in my imagination—for The Poet had told me no such thing—I'd decided that his one true love must have been some tough, sunburnt Israeli girl he'd met on that kibbutz twenty years ago, that he was an Irishman with a thing for Jewish women—and here I was, a Jewish girl from New York who'd so effectively pretended to be Irish.

Yes, I was ridiculous. Dublin had been good to me; it had given me everything I had wanted of it and more. And my thanks was to cry over someone who had not, when I thought about it, broken my heart. Who had meant, I understood, only to be honest with me. And there, on the bridge, I laughed at my pride and foolishness, and I thought of the sad, unforgettable last line of Joyce's great story "Araby," in which a young Dubliner, in the painful dawning of self-awareness, says, "Gazing up into the darkness I saw myself as a creature driven and derided by vanity; and my eyes burned with anguish and anger." I didn't have it *that* bad.

As my own misguided anguish abated, I continued my march back to Trinity, past the lampposts where The Poet and I had kissed only hours before, the same shuttered pubs, the same Georgian buildings. To the college gates, where I knocked loudly and one of the guards let me in. "Haven't seen you in a spell," one said.

"Been busy." I was drenched, and I'm sure he could tell I'd been crying.

"Right-o," he said sympathetically. "You get some sleep then."

I got some sleep. And I knew I'd be okay. I still had Ryan. And Grogan's. I still had my young Socialist comrades. I still had Guinness. I still had Jameson. That weekend, I went west to Galway, just as native Dubliners so often do when they need to get away, clear their heads, sort things out. I drank a lot of whiskey and flirted with a lot of strangers. I slept with an English backpacker in a narrow squeaky cot at the youth hostel. It was true; American girls were easy. I felt better.

And, it turned out, I still had The Poet. Within days of my return to Dublin, I had more or less moved back in with him. Things were different, and, in a way, better. We had an understanding. We were friends. We drank our whiskey at night, our tea in the morning. We shared a bed. We talked. I even switched my return flight to extend my stay in Ireland two more weeks, pushing it as close to the beginning of the school year in Vermont as I could. I didn't feel ready to leave Dublin, even though by then I had conceded that, no, I was not Irish after all. And that was just fine. It was also just fine not to be the most beloved, but loved enough.

4.

SHADOW SCHOOL

The Pig, North Bennington, Vermont

Poor Tessie Hutchinson. "It isn't fair, it isn't right," she protests at the end of Shirley Jackson's short story "The Lottery," that exquisite American Gothic miniature well known to anyone who took high school English in the United States between, roughly, 1950 and the present. No, it certainly isn't fair, isn't right: Tessie, having drawn the slip of paper with the telltale black dot, is about to become the latest victim of a savage annual tradition—a human sacrifice—right there on the village green of her tiny New England hamlet. She is about to get stoned to death by her fellow townsfolk, her neighbors, her people. "The Lottery" is an exposure—distorted and magnified—not only of the brutality that lurks just beneath the serene surface of small-town life, but of the cruelty of which all people might just be capable.

This particular territory, where poor, fictional Tessie breathed her last, is familiar to me. The town in which "The Lottery" takes place is presumed to be modeled on North

Bennington, Vermont—where Jackson lived with her husband, the literary critic Stanley Edgar Hyman, who taught at Bennington College, the very small school situated just up the hill from the very small town. I've read that Jackson sometimes felt suffocated there, and often unwelcome, with four children to raise, a big weird messy house to run, and more talent and ambition than the role of faculty wife generally allowed for in her time.

It's well known that Jackson was fascinated by witchcraft, both in its literary and practical applications. She may have developed this interest before she settled in North Bennington, but it's just the sort of place where such a sensibility can, with little effort, completely take hold. Were witches ever tried and burned there? I doubt it. But I always felt that the spirit of the place smacked of the mystic. Every full moon loomed hugely over the campus and the nearby village, illuminating swarms of fearsome bats fluttering below. One especially gray and ominous midwinter afternoon, I could've sworn I saw a wolf driving a battered old station wagon up Main Street, even though upon reflection it was probably just a hairy guy, of which there is no shortage in Vermont. Whatever or whoever it was, I was spooked, irrationally or not. And then there were the woods, through which ran the shortest path from the village to the center of campus. What kind of forces, wicked or benevolent or neutral, mastered and animated this small forest I cannot say, but many mornings I paused at the start of the path to offer a quick but sincere prayer that I might pass safely through. I figured it couldn't hurt to ask. I am superstitious.

Those woods enchanted me, surely in no small part because they frightened me. Starting in my freshman year, I would repair to them frequently for solace, for comfort, for inspiration, for the hope they extended—a hope fed abundantly by a steady diet of Wordsworth and Yeats and Emerson and Frost—that in them I might make contact with the spirit of nature itself and, by Romantic-Transcendental extension, with God, whatever that might be. There in Vermont, in as much nature as a native New Yorker might ever dream possible, I felt both more deeply connected with the natural world than ever and more set apart from it—out of nature, *supernatural* in the sense I believe, perhaps mistakenly, to be most heartbreakingly literal. In my freshman and sophomore years, when I still lived on campus, my roommate grew accustomed to tense telephone exchanges with my intransigently cosmopolitan mother.

"Where is my daughter?" she would demand without so much as a prefatory "hello."

"She's in the woods," my roommate would answer.

"In the woods?" my mother would bellow. "She's from *New York*. She could get killed there. What is she doing *in the woods?*"

"Communing with nature. Or something. I'll let her know you called."

My mother knew, even as I wished to deny it, that the

woods were not where I belonged. It's true; I am a city person. And while North Bennington could hardly qualify as an urban environment, it offered at least some of the amenities of civilized life; namely, it had a bar.

But the thing about small towns is, *they are small.* People will know all your shit, and you will know theirs, and you, and they, will have to accept that. Commercially, this tiny pocket of northern North Americana had little to say for itself. It had a post office, a general store, a pizzeria, a fancy restaurant where your mom and dad might take you to dinner during parents' weekend or a friend might get a job bussing tables, a gas-station-slash-cigarette-and-beer-convenience store with launderette attached, a bank—and the bar. And there's no way that each and every day you spend in a small town, and pass your time and live your life in these few venues, you're not going to run into someone you know and who knows you. Unless you are an absolute shut-in—like Constance Blackwood in Jackson's great novel *We Have Always Lived in the Castle*—you cannot hide from your fellow townsfolk.

Certainly, as I sat on the front porch of my little first-floor apartment on the village's Main Street, I relished having a convenient vantage point from which to monitor the comings and goings at various hours of those whom I knew to live in North B, as most of us called it, and those whom I knew did not. I passed many temperate evenings on that shabby porch, playing Scrabble or cards with friends, maybe sharing a bottle of cheap wine or a six-pack of beer and a bag of chips, and many mornings with coffee and cigarettes and a crossword puzzle before going to class. From there I could observe an off-campus version of the well-known Walk of Shame on campus, where one might witness over weekend brunch the traffic patterns across the main lawn, and if you knew who lived where, as most of us did, well, you could arrive at all sorts of conclusions. Small, isolated places breed this kind of thinking.

It didn't take much doing to understand why Jackson had allegorized her little community in the most sinister way imaginable, but to a big-city girl like myself, North Bennington was also something new and nearly heavenly: all scuffed picket fences and hilly streets and beat-up clapboard-clad or brick houses that listed to one side or the other, lilac trees that burst into perfumed life every muddy spring, twisty creeks and canals that sang and sputtered. In autumn, Vermont may just be the most magnificent place on earth: its frantic display of so much red and orange and gold, its trees that bleed and flame with the splendor of incipient fatality. But otherwise, there's little grandeur to speak of in North Bennington, dotted as it is with rusty rotting mills and expired factories, sliced by railroad tracks upon which no trains have rolled since God remembers when. North B isn't stately like neighboring Old Bennington, with its neoclassical mansions and phallic-triumphalist obelisk commemorating the Battle of Bennington (which actually took place a town west, in Hoosick, New York), its whitewashed, austere Congregational church and its picturesque graveyard in which generations of students have paid their drunken midnight respects at the grave of Robert Frost. North B is also too settled to be called bucolic. Still, it's charming in its own modest way; it is humble, it is ordinary, a small town populated by families and working people, a handful of college professors, and the few students, like myself, lucky enough to get permission to live off campus. I moved to North B as fast as I could, first into the only college-owned off-campus house—a gray Victorian cube capped by a cupola, just beyond the railroad tracks—and then into the Main Street apartment with the front porch the summer before my senior year.

Bennington College regarded itself at the time as a "self-selecting" school, which may have been just a friendly and parent-comforting way of saying it wasn't hard to get into. They had let me in, after all—a high school dropout with math SAT scores, my brother quipped, that probably wouldn't have gotten me into the National Hockey League. But by then I badly wanted to be a student, and, I hoped, a good one. I wanted to read lots of books and, seduced by the glossy catalog the college had sent along with an application for admission and which I pored over dreamily for many weeks, I envisioned myself hauling great stacks of important literary works across the idyllic campus, trudging through piles of crunchy fallen leaves in hiking boots until I ran into a fellow student, maybe even a professor, and we launched into an impromptu argument about the last novels of Henry James, or about third-world feminist poetry, or something else about which I knew nothing. I wanted to write lots of papers (even if I would chronically turn them in late). I wanted to learn. I entered college in the fall of 1990, about two years after dropping out of high school, a time I'd spent mostly following the Grateful Dead around the country. Because I'd been out of school for a while, I thought of myself, at the ripe old age of nineteen, as a "mature" freshman.

In a way, that was true. For me, college was not my first taste of freedom, but instead a chance to redeem myself, to un-fuck-up as best I could. I was over drugs, but drinking had already become a part of who I was. The one little bar in North B was a major draw to off-campus life. It was the only one within reasonable walking distance of school, and living in town would bring me even closer. I liked my classes, I idolized my professors, I joined about a half-dozen committees. But on campus, socially, I felt dislocated.

When I first visited the bar in North Bennington, as a sophomore, it was still called the Villager, and most everybody called it the V. Seniors, graduate students, and a few professors drank there. And not everybody who spent time there was involved with the college, which gave the students who hung out there a different, more intimate perspective on life in this depressed corner of New England. There were guys like Alex and Adrian, who'd graduated from

Bennington in the previous decade but had stuck around
and were now more Vermont than Vermonters. And there
was a fantastic bartender with a huge, warm laugh, who also
happened to be a fine poet. This was where I wanted to be,
more than at campus parties. It felt more like how I imagined
the real world felt like, and I knew that college wasn't the real
world.

By the time I was a senior, the Villager had twice changed
ownership and names. For about one miserable year, it was a
mediocre restaurant with delusions of grandeur. The new
owners made it clear that students were not welcome, no
matter how un-studently we behaved. It wanted skiers, it
wanted tourists, it wanted anyone but us. The owner eyed us
with suspicion whenever we sat down at the bar. She was
foolish, because in such a small town, a bar's bread and butter is bound to be the locals, and in this case, the locals
included students. Predictably the venture failed, and soon
enough, two lovable middle-aged sisters from the Berkshires
took over the space and opened an unpretentious bar and
restaurant where all (of legal drinking age) were welcome.

It was a refreshing and necessary change of guard following an unpleasant and distressing interlude, and it struck
many of us that the sisters' only misstep was in the name
they'd chosen to bestow upon their establishment. They
renamed it No Baloney, a disconcerting fact that one could
not ignore, proclaimed as it was on the sign they hung outside the premises; a sign embellished, no less, by the smiling

visage of a plump pink pig. Those of us who had wasted no time establishing ourselves as regulars took to calling it the Pig Bar, and often, even more efficiently, the Pig. Despite this, it was a wonderfully civilized little place. And as dreadful as its real name was, it had a ring of truth and rectitude: There *was* no baloney here, no BS, no airs or fripperies. The food was good in a standard and honest way, the drinks were reasonably priced, the atmosphere unfussy.

After Grogan's in Dublin, the Pig became my second proper local. There, a small group of friends—including a handful of male professors—drank and talked until late most every night. And among the regulars who were not connected with the college, none was more regular than Stan—a sweet, funny sap of a man who worked at the local auto parts shop. And among the faculty, there was no one whose company I kept more often than David, a professor of English literature.

His prodigious drinking habits were the source of not a little gossip and awe on campus. Everybody had heard about the time he had instructed the students in a Beckett seminar to show up at his house to watch a film, and how we banged on his door and called him on the telephone for the better part of the morning until he finally was able to lift himself from his drunkbed, open the door, let us in, and screen the movie. (There was also a rumor, which I never quite believed, that he had passed a student in a previous Beckett seminar who had submitted, as his or her final paper, twenty blank sheets of paper.) None of this demonstrably diminished the quality of his teaching, which was engaging and challenging. He was a tall, lanky, pallid character, handsome in a dissolute, faintly Byronic way.

His intellect was formidable and, to me, anyway, intimidating in its breadth and its rigor. He had a sharp and confident, if not downright arrogant, discursive style that lent itself well to debates, in which he habitually prevailed. As with the woods, I was drawn to him because I was a little bit afraid of him—for all of his cultivation, I still detected a streak of wildness about him—and I was certain that I stood to gain much from his company, if I could muster the nerve to keep it.

And if one drinks, at least sometimes, to try to forget one's worries, well, he had plenty reason to drink (not that he needed one): A big shift was underway on campus. A beloved faculty member had been unceremoniously canned more than a year earlier, and the need for further faculty cuts had been announced—an assessment that, to many students and professors, seemed less than perfectly honest. During my sophomore year, I had been one of the instigators of a student insurgency orchestrated to obtain the economic evidence that such cuts were in fact necessary; many students suspected that something other than a fiscal shortfall was behind the cuts, that the administration regarded a good number of instructors as enemies, that this was a matter of academic freedom under threat. Our well-intended but

naively planned student takeover of the college president's
and other administrative offices failed to yield the evidence,
or lack thereof, we'd sought. We thought we'd been pretty
savvy, but in our youthful cluelessness, we had never antici-
pated that the president and her partisans in the administration would refuse to give us what we wanted, and we had
failed to consider the paramount importance of having a
strong exit strategy. If our student protest did little to protect
the jobs of those whose jobs we wished to protect, it did
bring some of us closer to our professors and fortify our alli-
ance. They could be sure that we were on their side.

Bennington had long been known as a place where teachers and students were pretty cozy. Everyone was on a
first-name basis. It was not unheard of for teachers to show
up at big campus parties, nor was it uncommon for them to
invite their students over for dinner. A strange and wonderful professor of something called experimental music per-
mitted students to write our own evaluations, believing that
even if we failed to materialize as scheduled in his classroom,
it didn't matter, because surely we had to be somewhere
learning something anyway, even if that somewhere was still
in bed with a pounding headache and that something was
this: tequila followed by Jägermeister was an incredibly stupid idea. My father's objections to my matriculation at Bennington were numerous and voluble. He was a Cornell man

like his father before him, and Bennington—with no grades, few tests, no sports teams save intramural coed soccer and volleyball—didn't quite strike him as a *real* college like his own. And, gallingly, the cost of tuition was higher. Moreover, he recalled a journalist crony who'd taught there in the 1980s and often returned to New York on the weekends with stories of conquests among the young women of the college; whether they were true or just so much bogus bravado, they made an impression.

Many evenings at the Pig my senior year, I could be found ensconced at the bar or at a table in David's company, maybe with a few other students, and maybe another professor and other regulars. David drank Scotch or martinis, and when we weren't talking about campus politics, we might be talking about poetry. I was writing my senior thesis on Yeats, an endeavor undertaken with the earnest, focused seriousness of purpose one hopes might also be devoted to international peace summits. Looking back, it was a wildly convoluted mishmash of ideas: I'd set out to try to figure out what Yeats was doing with Irish folklore in his earliest and last poems, but what kept popping up in my reading and my thinking was that mostly his poems seemed to be about his troubles with the ladies. (You might know that when Maud Gonne declined Yeats's marriage proposal, he turned next to her daughter, who also shot him down. Maybe you're even aware of what he'd been up to with monkey glands; I'm not going to go into that here.) But since I was pretty sure I couldn't be awarded a degree—even at Bennington—for writing about Yeats not getting any, I called it his *sublimation of desire*. And if all that weren't enough, I was sure Yeats couldn't quite figure out what to make of himself, and this I called *the unmasking of poetic identity*. Ah, youth.

Although David was not my thesis advisor and Yeats was not his field, because he knew something about everything, and that included modern Irish poetry, he would indulge me, at the bar, in impromptu Yeats recitations. His big number was "A Last Confession," which he delivered with great feeling and beauty:

What lively lad most pleasured me
Of all that with me lay?
I answer that I gave my soul
And loved in misery,
But had great pleasure with a lad
That I loved bodily.

Flinging from his arms I laughed
To think his passion such
He fancied that I gave a soul
Did but our bodies touch,
And laughed upon his breast to think
Beast gave beast as much.

I gave what other women gave
That stepped out of their clothes.
But when this soul, its body off,
Naked to naked goes,
He it has found shall find therein
What none other knows,

And give his own and take his own
And rule in his own right;
And though it loved in misery
Close and cling so tight,
There's not a bird of day that dare
Extinguish that delight.

I regret that I never asked him why *this*, why this poem, out of them all. It's a sad number, but it is also strong and defiant, and forcefully erotic. And Yeats wrote other poems in the voice of a woman—most famously the ones spoken by the truth-telling madwoman Crazy Jane. What exactly this poem says about intimacy remains mysterious to me, even after hundreds of readings. Here, the desire is hardly sublimated; it is right there on the surface. And here, it cannot be ignored, misery and pleasure are coupled. The woods of North Bennington. That poem. And David himself. Three things I loved, and feared.

As for myself, I'd launch into one of the poems with which my thinking, at the time, had been most occupied: the dreamy, sexy call of the faerie folk in "The Hosting of the Sidhe," the mournful antiheroics of "Cuchulain Comforted," or the late-period reckoning of "The Circus Animals' Desertion," with its irresistible big finish in the foul rag-and-bone shop of the heart, all of which I had committed to memory. When I recall my favorite nights at the Pig, I recall reciting—and discussing—poems with David, and, even better, I recall David flattering me by saying that I was one of the only students he could treat like an adult. No utterance could have pleased me more.

But when we weren't reciting or talking about poetry, David and I were talking about campus politics, or I was nervously trying to hold up my end of arguments about topics he'd chosen, about which he certainly knew more, about which he held far more confident and lucid and interesting opinions. I was in college during the height of the culture wars—this was when Antioch College, a school that shared a progressive history with Bennington, became the focus of national attention for its sexual offense prevention policy, in which, at least as the many parodies would have it, every step on the path to seduction required direct questions (May I touch your arm? Would you take offense if I told you I found you attractive? etc.), and questions of freedom of speech had taken on considerable urgency. But he would quickly tire of discussions of the matter and ask instead why people focused so much on free speech and not enough on freedom of representation. This proved prescient when, that same year, an exhibit of student work in a small gallery outside the college president's office was censored and finally taken down—a state of affairs so contrary to what many of us believed was the spirit of the college that it confirmed our feeling that the school was betraying its own principles.

Another, and far trickier, favorite riff for late-night drunken debate was abortion. David seemed to think that students' arguments in its favor were weak and softheaded, and wouldn't it be much more interesting, really, if we just conceded that it was in fact a kind of murder, and then produce some smart way to justify both? Whenever it came up, and it came up often, I'd squirm uncomfortably on my barstool until I landed on something to say, to which he'd respond by shaking his head and saying, "Can't you be more clever?" And then, stinging, "I thought I could treat you like an adult."

There was nothing I wanted more than to be more clever and to be treated, especially by David, like an adult, and I hated to disappoint. I often thought that if he ever tired of teaching, he would have made a fine district attorney. In my college classes, I was getting an excellent education in English literature, in critical theory, in becoming a good reader. But these off-hours arguments to which I felt so ill-prepared to contribute, far from the more ordered world of the classroom, were like a shadow university. In them, I got another kind of education altogether, one that would help prepare me for a future full of the kind of whiskey-fueled conversations that come up not infrequently when one spends a good portion of one's life in bars and one is not able to determine and control the subjects that arise in such circumstances, unless one wishes to be deemed a windbag, a control freak, or some other variety of undesirable. If you don't want to talk, you might as well stay at home and drink and not bother with bars. But if you're at the bar, brace yourself: You might be called upon to argue in favor of cannibalism, or recount the history of the Bull Moose Party, or make NFL draft predictions. (I have since been involved in barroom discussions of all three.) You never know. And that's one of the great pleasures of drinking in bars.

And this is nothing new. "The role of the saloon as a popular forum for the exchange of news and views was a continuation of a centuries-old function of tavern culture dating back to medieval England and before," writes historian Madelon Powers in *Faces Along the Bar*. She continues, "In succeeding centuries . . . people of all classes made increasing use of drinking establishments as marketplaces for ideas. For example, Samuel Johnson, the noted literary critic, was an habitué of the Turk's Head Tavern in London in the eighteenth century. In his words, 'wine there exhilarates my spirits, and prompts me to free conversation and an interchange of discourse with those whom I most love: I dogmatise and am contradicted, and in this conflict of opinions I find delight.'" The flow of discourse in Bennington's classrooms was often stimulating; at the bar—a few whiskeys into a long night—it was even better.

Winter, senior year, I stayed in my apartment in North Bennington to continue writing about Yeats instead of taking an internship in a big city during the two-month period, as most students did. During this span, student life seemed more distant than ever—despite the big stacks of books on my desk—and I felt like just any other person who lived in a small town, frequenting its sole bar, shopping in its only grocery store, mailing letters and catching up on local news at the tiny post office near the railroad tracks. With few fellow students around during the break—which was called Field Work Term—those of us who stayed behind closed ranks even further and relied on one another for support and for relief from the isolation which, though lovely much of the time, could also become hard to bear throughout the short cold days and long, dark, even colder nights.

The walls of my living room had been painted by the previous tenant a grotesque shade of rosy pink that looked to me much like the interior of a mouth or, I imagined, a womb. Too broke and lazy and otherwise preoccupied to repaint it, I accepted it and even came to love it; it conferred a feeling of warmth that my barely heated apartment badly needed. I'd spend most of my days in that pink room, listening to Billy Bragg or the Pogues or weepy old folk songs or the local public radio station, going over Yeats's poems line by line and word by word, cultivating some sense of their worth and meaning as I also slowly developed a sense of the sort of person I wished to be when I grew up—a person a great deal like some of my favorite professors, I imagined, maybe even as witty and conversant as David—even if that still felt distant and a little painful to think on. I'd make big cheap pots of soup with lentils and too many spices, and many evenings— after a few whiskeys at the Pig—my friend Rachel would come over and we'd bundle ourselves in sweaters and blankets and eat that hippie soup and drink herbal tea and talk until late late late about books and politics. And boys.

On politics and books and art, we were pretty simpatico. On the boy front, however, Rachel was doing a lot better—or worse, depending on how you looked at it—than I was. They were, at least, a serious part of her life—even if they added up to a whole lot of heartache. I had little going on to speak of in that department, and even if I sometimes fretted about that, my hybrid student-townie life mostly felt full and satisfying and provided enough distractions. The men whose company I kept were a few close friends, gay and straight, a few professors, the local guys at the Pig, and the graduate sculpture students who hung out at the bar, too—young men who liked to break things and build things and use power tools and play with fire, and who were the closest thing to jocks the college had.

Occasionally I would find myself in the predicament of

having a little crush on one or another of them, and I'd just try to shake it off and clear my head and get back to the more important business of Yeats and Wordsworth and Blake and philosophy and anthropology and the literary magazine and student activism. I couldn't be bothered with that boy crap, and I had accepted that I was in an environment in which the competition for that kind of attention from the opposite sex was unusually strong: Not only did girls outnumber guys by a pretty wide margin, but I don't think I'm exaggerating when I report that among the female population in the student body, the percentage of women who were extraordinarily pretty, stylish, and smart was extremely high. And I wonder if, having gotten the sense early on that I really couldn't compete, I opted out of the game altogether. For my last solid year or so of college, I'd cultivated an androgynous look that relied heavily upon a tweed suit that I wore just about every other day and oxblood oxfords when the weather didn't call for all-terrain monster hiking boots. I knew that something was missing, but I wasn't up to the task of figuring out exactly what that something was, much less trying to get it. I tried to sort it out in a poem:

> The bar closes, the students disband. Some, arm in arm.
> Others laugh, and sing the chorus of a folk song whose meaning
> They had abandoned at the campfire before adolescence.
> These are not comrades. And none will say the words that matter
> Above all others; the ones that are true are locked in the heart.

Outside, the cold and the stars and the rain and the pavement
Are content with their own speechlessness. And a girl
Walks home alone; there has been something left unsaid.
She clicks on the television, turns down the volume.
She falls into an unmade bed, kicks her shoes to the floor.

When she rises fully dressed in the previous evening's clothes,
In the same dress that, too, had refused to say what it meant,
She cannot remember her dreams. The television is still on.
The newspaper brings no news, and the dishes remain unwashed.
A failure of language; the return of the unfinished page.

Reading it now, all these years later, of course it makes me cringe a little. So maybe I wasn't as good at sublimating desire, or at making poems, as I thought I was. And of course it's only in retrospect that I see that I spent a year writing about how Yeats was sublimating desire, pouring my young and earnest heart into it, without once stopping and thinking, *Oh fuck, me too, maybe that's also exactly what I'm doing.* Night after night, I went out and drank, sometimes in the company of men who liked me a whole lot, but they didn't love me, not in that way, anyway, and with others whose quick wit and encyclopedic intelligence intimidated me, hard as I tried, and sometimes managed, to keep up with them.

The same winter, I came down with what I assumed was just an especially vicious cold. Chills, fever, fluorescent greenish snot, hacking cough, the works. Still, I persisted in my usual routine of eating poorly, drinking heavily, and chain-smoking. My friends at the bar expressed concern. I told them I'd be fine. But it got so bad that I wasn't even able to drag my ass down the street to the Pig. I was home, alone, self-medicating with aspirin and Robitussin and whatever other promising antihistamines or decongestants or expectorants happened to be at hand, and hot whiskey with lemon and honey and cloves. I tried to keep doing my work, but I could hardly focus on reading. My head was so heavy, I could barely stay awake.

One night, about a week into this affliction, I started to drift into sleep. But before my eyes fully closed, I heard a voice speaking softly. "Don't. Lie. Down," it said calmly but gravely. At first I panicked. Had my time in this small village turned me into one of those isolated, unwell young women right out of a Shirley Jackson story? What kind of freaky North Bennington witchcraft was this?

Bleary and worried, I turned to see who was speaking to me, and there, by my bedside, was a small fuzzy lamb with the face of William Blake. Naturally, I relaxed.

It is likely that the combination of over-the-counter drugs and Jameson made this visitation possible, but it was nonetheless perfectly real. And if it wasn't just an episode for which alcohol and pharmacology were responsible, then I was willing to chalk it up to the weird, strong magic of North Bennington working upon me, and I could not ignore it. I did exactly as the William Blake lamb implored me, and instead of lying down, I propped myself up on a pile of pillows such that, when I did finally allow myself to sleep, I was nearly sitting upright.

The next day, one of the sisters who owned the bar called. "Honey, you need to get yourself to the emergency room," she said. "We know you're sick, and we're worried." I was nearly delirious by then. A friend came and picked me up and took me to the ER, where I was told I had a pretty advanced case of pneumonia. In telling me not to lie down, that William Blake lamb-apparition-hallucination may have saved my life. It's not uncommon, I was told, for people with pneumonia to choke in their sleep on phlegm. Antibiotics replaced all the other crap I'd been taking, I managed to lay off the cigs for a spell, and the sisters from the bar and other friends from the Pig brought soup and checked in on me until I was well.

Even more than Grogan's in Dublin, my life at the Pig gave me a sense of how powerful the fellowship among bar regulars could be, how the people one drank with could, in a way, fill in for family. This does not square with depictions of bars in popular culture. The power of Richard Brooks's film *Looking for Mr. Goodbar* as a cultural touchstone is fading now, more than thirty years after it was released, though it still attracts a cult following. But it was strong enough in my college days that when my mother (who had nothing against a good bar herself) became aware that I spent quite a lot of time at a bar, she urged me to see it, as though it might foretell what terrible fate awaited me if I didn't watch myself.

The film, laden with hazy, hallucinatory flashbacks and heavy-handed symbolism, is based on Judith Rossner's novel, which was in turn inspired by the terrible true story of New York City schoolteacher Roseann Quinn. Diane Keaton plays Theresa Dunn—dedicated, talented teacher of deaf children by day, sex-and-drug-and-booze-addled bar cruiser by night. We learn that she is the daughter of an oppressive Catholic father; that she was confined to a body cast as a child; that she doesn't quite measure up to her glamorous (but equally troubled) sister. All this is meant to explain the self-hatred that leads to her risky behavior. At her local haunt, she picks up men—the more violent, the better—and takes them home with her. In the end, she is brutally murdered—as her real-life counterpart Quinn was in 1973—by one such man, a psychopathic drifter.

In it, there is no semblance of the bar culture I had come to love—but its cautionary tenor and prurient moralizing certainly did not escape me. Do terrible things ever happen to women at bars? Of course they do. But at one little public house in small-town Vermont, I told my worried mother, I encountered no danger, no sexual peril. Instead, there were people who cared about my well-being, and, on one crucial occasion, delivered soup to my door.

The sisters' intervention surely had as much to do with

my return to health as the English Romantic lamb by my
bedside. I knew that I could count on my friends at the Pig,
not least on the sisters, who'd even hired me to pitch in as a
bartender from time to time, which I loved as much as I loved
being on the other side of the bar. To tend bar at the only
place within walking distance of one's school confers a great
sense of power and privilege: I could demand to take professors' car keys away from them, and decline to serve anyone I
knew to be underage. It also felt like a kind of ministry, for it
is true that people like to pour their hearts out to sympathetic barkeeps, and I was nothing if not sympathetic. I only
wished I could be more helpful. What to do for Stan of the
auto repair goods store when he lamented his loneliness?
What to do when teachers and other adults I respected spoke
of dissatisfaction and worry? Not much except listen—and
that, I knew, counted for something. When I was broke or
hungry or lonely, or a little bit of each, I knew I would always
be taken care of at the bar by its people, and I would be there
for them, too.

As graduation approached, terror crept in. What on earth
would I do with the rest of my life? Where would I go?
As diligently as I'd worked on my Yeats project, I was afraid
I wouldn't finish it. I had a few other final papers to write,
and I didn't think I'd be able to get my work done. And that
meant I wouldn't graduate. And I wonder, especially in

retrospect, if maybe I didn't *want* to graduate. I'd done plenty of complaining in my four years of college. I'd threatened to drop out many times. (Second semester sophomore year had been a particularly low point. I told one of my professors—a super cool jazz trumpeter—that I intended to take a bus from Montreal to Managua, where I'd maybe meet a nice Sandinista and live in a hammock for the rest of my days. "It doesn't matter where you go," he said to me. "If you're carrying around a big sack of shit, you'll still have a big sack of shit when you get there.") But my two years off-campus, where it had been so easy to pretend that I was just a regular almost-adult who happened to commute up the hill to a job that happened to be going to school, had been pretty great. I liked that life. I liked my pink womb of an apartment, the hilly streets and the little lake nearby, the fresh air, and the starry night sky. And I loved my bar, where in the sisters I found surrogate moms who accepted and cared about me.

But I had to graduate. I'd dropped out before. I'd never much worried about being a minor disgrace and disappointment to my real family, but now, a little older, I did worry a little about disappointing myself—and the teachers whose respect and faith I had somehow managed to earn. Someday, I had to finish *something*. I could easily imagine being like certain friends from the bar: I could ease into a simple life in southwestern Vermont, find some kind of job, stay forever . . .

But I did finish, even though as the end of the term

approached, it didn't seem possible. I sat at my desk until the early hours of the morning, finishing my thesis and the other papers that were due, drinking pot after pot of strong tea, occasionally answering the door when friends from the bar dropped by to make sure I'd eaten something, to make sure I was okay. I handed in my work at the last possible minute, and I graduated.

When graduation day arrived and I was handed a college diploma, I actually felt kind of proud of myself. Maybe I had shaken off my proclivity for being a fuckup. I doubted it, but maybe I was finally heading in the right direction.

At the same time, God, was I sad. It was likely that I'd never—or, at best, rarely—see the sisters and my other friends from the Pig once I moved on. I might stay in touch with David and the other professors with whom I'd been close, but the four-year life cycle of college meant that they'd have other students to teach—and to meet at the bar for drinks and arguments.

As a compromise, I gave myself the gift of one final summer in North Bennington, its gentle hills and small-town comforts, its trees and streams and fresh air and distinct magic. I had to move on. I knew that. But I couldn't tear myself away so suddenly. Not from that bar. Not from those woods. And at summer's end, on my last morning in Vermont, I stopped again at the path's threshold and asked for safe passage, as I had on so many mornings during the previous years. But that day, I didn't walk through the woods; I no longer had any reason, any need, to go to campus. Instead, I walked back to my apartment, taped up the last few boxes of books, swept the floor, moved my stuff out to the front porch where I waited for the U-Haul to arrive, and locked the door behind me.

5

HOW TO BEHAVE IN A BAR

The Man of Kent, Hoosick Falls, New York

One of America's greatest bars is located in the unheralded town of Hoosick Falls, New York, a small working class community about an hour east of Albany. It was established by and, until the summer of 2007, presided over by John—an incomparable, tough-tender former merchant seaman, uranium miner, dockworker, and all-around first-class bloke from Kent, England, who had rescued a three-legged cat, kept ducks and geese and even a pig named Millie in the yard, stocked more than a hundred varieties of beer between the taps and bottles, and ensured that everyone felt safe and happy, well watered and well fed on his watch. To call his bar, the Man of Kent, a roadhouse isn't exactly right, but its location, on a country road, smack-dab in the middle of nowhere, lends it some unmistakably roadhousey properties, and makes it a favored oasis not just for skiers on their way from New York City to the slopes of Vermont, but especially for bikers tearing through New England. If you don't know it's there, it's pretty easy to miss, even with the folksy hand-painted sign of a country gentleman in hunting clothes posted outside. Driving by, it looks like a modest low-slung house with an exuberantly planted front garden and large terrace.

It took some doing to get there, but I went to the Man of Kent whenever I could. I don't think *anyone* lived within walking distance of the Man of Kent, except for John and his American wife, just next door. It's about twenty minutes by car from Bennington along twisty and often treacherous Route 7, past the Tomhannock Reservoir, and I didn't drive then and still don't. Besides, even if I did drive, I'd never be able to make it back from that bar in one piece after a few Belgian beers and maybe a whiskey or two. Getting there was easiest if one had a designated driver at the ready, and I sometimes had one in my straight-edge punk-rock friend Theo, who was happy to transport his friends to the Man of Kent, then bring us safely home.

It was the perfect respite from campus; it was a treat, a proper night out. To go to this roadside inn on a chilly night, having made the journey on this dark, winding road, was to step not quite into the past, but into a place that felt as though it existed outside of time. Even coming from not so far away, I felt like a weary traveler at the end of a journey, grateful for warmth and shelter, for safety and good company.

The atmosphere was unlike anywhere else around, brightly lit—ludicrously bright, really, but you got used to it—and kitted out in British memorabilia: rugby and soccer jerseys, cricket gear, legions of terrycloth bar towels advertising Fuller's and Young's and Old Speckled Hen, and other bits of Anglocentric flotsam and jetsam I was not yet prepared to identify when I first visited as a college sophomore. There was a television, but it never dominated; despite the trappings, this was no sports bar. There was no jukebox, but there was always a sound track: John was especially fond of World War II–era English music-hall standards and French chanteurs and chanteuses. For all its blazing brightness, for all its kitsch, it still had everything that great bars have: a strong sense of itself, a superb and commanding presence behind the bar, in John, and a mix of people, young and old, rich and not rich and in between. And clearly, what made John happiest was playing host, in a protective and almost paternal way, to that diverse blend of patrons: local people in flannels and fleeces and heavy hiking boots whose families had lived in the area for generations, professors and students from the few colleges nearby or close enough (Bennington and Rensselaer Polytechnic and the State University at Albany), and the tourists who traversed Route 7 year after year, skiers on their way to the slopes of Vermont from New York City, and those gangs of bikers—some weekend warriors in shiny new leathers on shiny new bikes, some scary-ass old-school dudes with forbidding tattoos and wild hair held back by bandannas, with faces that never cracked smiles and their beloved Harleys parked outside, for many of whom the Man of Kent was a final pit stop before zooming across the narrow southern end of Vermont to hasten to the promised land of New Hampshire, where they could LIVE FREE OR DIE on roads that might not have been totally lawless, but at least did not demand the indignity of helmets.

To me, the place seemed curiously genteel for the Born to Be Wild crowd, but they loved being there. And that's because John made everyone feel right at home: As long as you minded your manners, didn't make trouble, were at least a *little* friendly, you were cool with him. The bikers could be daunting, but no one dared start any trouble in John's bar. It wasn't so much that he actively brokered peace among the different groups; it was more implicit. For a very nice man, he also had just enough of the tough guy about him, solid and barrel-chested, to make it perfectly clear that you'd best behave yourself. He didn't mind a little boisterous inebriated good cheer—even a table full of sloppy singing students could get an indulgent nod—but it was understood that if you crossed the line, you might just be in for it. No one wanted to be on this man's bad side.

When I went there with fellow students who weren't as bar-savvy as others, who were new to the place, I made sure to tell them in advance that John was wonderful but formidable, and he wouldn't put up with any crap in his bar. "Be nice," I'd tell them, "be respectful." And since in the area

Bennington students had a not-wholly-undeserved reputation for being entitled, I had made it something of a personal
mission to demonstrate that not all of us were like that. Campus parties were the best and safest places to behave like a
moron, if that's what you wanted, and many did. But at the
Man of Kent, you had to be on your best behavior. And if
you'd established yourself as a known entity and turned up
with a group of newcomers, you understood tacitly that the
group was your responsibility, that its behavior was a reflection of your own character.

There are ways to behave, and not to behave, in bars, and
each bar makes its own demands. There are loud bars where
conversation is not a priority, where cheap shots and cheaper
draft beer prevail, where the idea is to get drunk and not to
engage in any remotely complex way with your fellow patrons.
There are quiet bars, lit low and engineered for tête-à-têtes.
And at the Man of Kent, which was neither of those things,
but a place both brightly festive and undeniably civilized,
where students were invariably outnumbered by proper
adults, I started to understand, with greater clarity than ever,
how to behave in a bar.

After a youth marked by minor delinquency and chronic
insubordination, I had nonetheless emerged with good manners (though I can't say that I recall ever being taught them).
My mother sent mixed messages about the treatment of waiters and waitresses and bartenders and others who worked in

the service industry. She was often charming and generous, but at other times she was imperious, outrageously demanding, and sometimes downright mean. She once sent a cheeseburger back to the kitchen at a poolside café in Florida at least three times—growing more and more impatient, and contemptuous of the unfortunate waitress, whose fault it couldn't possibly have been, with each inadequate specimen—until it was precisely medium-rare, while my brother and I shrank deeper and deeper into our chairs, mortified. No matter how unhappy I was with my food or drink, I never wanted to treat anyone like that.

Still, it was going to the Man of Kent that showed me how to engage with bartenders. Certainly, I got along great with everyone at the bar in North Bennington—but they were my friends, part of my community, my substitute family, and I was there so often that they must have gotten used to all of my moods—good, bad, outgoing, withdrawn, celebratory, grouchy—and accepted all of them, as family must. It was more like an extension of my home than a separate place.

The impoliteness shown to bartenders is often appalling. Some patrons barely even acknowledge them, just bark out drink orders. Next time you're at a bar, just observe how many people even bother to say please and thank you. It will be less than half. And another thing: No matter how polite one is, one should never feel entitled to free drinks. A bartender does not have to give anyone anything. A third drink does not automatically mean the fourth is a buyback. But your chances of getting a drink—or two or more—on the house are vastly improved by being the kind of person who adds something to the life of the bar. It could be as simple as friendliness to the people on either side of you. It could be a good story. If you contribute to the culture of the bar in some way, the bar will want to keep you around. Never *ask* for a freebie. That's up to the bartender—not you. (As one Brooklyn barman I know memorably put it, "Buybacks are like blow jobs. If you have to ask for one, you don't deserve one.")

As for tipping, tip well. There are people who have tipped a dollar a drink for the past twenty years, as though bartenders are somehow immune to inflation. They aren't. Still, tipping well isn't the most important issue as a bar patron; it's attitude. If you're kind and calm and make a point of establishing eye contact, a bartender will take note, even in a crowded room. If you're impatient—shouting and brandishing cash—a bartender will also take note, but not in a good way. (I wouldn't have wanted to see someone wave money at John.) Patience, within reasonable limits, always pays off in a pub.

Occasionally, no matter how well everybody behaved, things could get a little rowdy at the Man of Kent. The biker/boho combo could be uneasy, regardless of John's protective, pacifying presence. One night, I showed up there wearing a hat a friend had recently given me—an absurd, multicolored, knobby knitted thing, somewhere between a skullcap and a tea cozy. I was with a bunch of friends from school, and we found a big empty table at the back. Going in, you couldn't *not* notice the cluster of bikers up front at the bar. These were not Bostonian lawyers roughing it for the weekend. These were real bikers: grizzled, packed into crusty jeans and reptilian chaps, T-shirts with Harley-Davidson logos and skulls and flames, leather vests, and huge boots, an unholy congregation of dirty denim and scuffed cowhide. Their hair was unkempt. The facial hair even more so. It looked like a casting call for a biopic about Motörhead's Lemmy.

John came around and took our order. I ordered a Belgian lambic—something I never did anywhere else, but the semisweet, semisour, strong beer with a hint of black cherry always tasted perfect there. Most of my friends had some kind of English ale or other. John made no comment about my hat. But a couple of those bikers were staring me down. "Maybe one of them wants to ask you out," my friend Owen cracked. It seemed unlikely.

We kept drinking and I tried to ignore the bikers. But there they were, at the opposite end of the room, staring. I felt perfectly safe, just a little weirded out. As long as John was there, nothing really bad could happen. I had another beer.

Soon enough, one of those bikers was ambling toward me, slowly and deliberately; not quite menacing, but walking like he was making a point of it, coming right at me. In my mind, the Vera Lynn or Charles Aznavour or whatever John had been playing had muted, and I was suddenly hearing a little Ennio Morricone, maybe something from *The Good, the Bad, and the Ugly*. Some of my friends looked like they were frozen in place. What did this guy want? He was big. Not the biggest of the bunch, but big. And though I had no idea what he was after, there was no mistaking that he meant business. He folded his arms into a defensive pretzel and looked me right in the eyes. "Ma'am," he said, his voice predictably gruff, but surprisingly soft at the same time.

Did he just ma'am *me?* I was in my early twenties, and he had to be an old man of, shit, at least thirty-five. I had never been *ma'am*ed before. He was just trying to be polite, I figured. Or maybe he was Southern.

"Yes?"

"You see my buddy back there?" He glanced over at the bar, at an older guy, the biggest of them all, maybe the leader of the gang—a great, imposing, black-leather-swaddled giant. How could I miss him?

"Yes."

"He really likes your hat." He backed up a little. "I mean, I like it, too," he said, "but my friend over there; he *really* likes it."

"Well, tell him I say thanks."

"The thing is," the biker continued, "he likes your hat so much, I think he *wants* it. And I'd like to get it for him. So how much you want for it?"

How much do I want for it? How exactly does one put a dollar value on such a thing? And was I being threatened?

Would there be consequences if I refused? Maybe he would not take no for an answer. My friends watched speechlessly. It seemed wise that they not chime in.

"Listen," I told the biker, "I can't sell it. It was a gift from a friend. And you know it's cold up here. I *need* this hat."

"All right, ma'am. I understand." And he skulked away, shoulders slumped.

John came around and took our order for another round. "Everything's all right, love?" he asked. He'd observed the proceedings from a distance. Nothing that happened at the Man of Kent escaped John's observation.

"Yeah, everything's fine," I said. "Thanks."

And everything *was* fine—at least for another ten minutes or so, when the guy approached me again. "Listen," he said, with not a little urgency in his tone. "My buddy really, *really* likes your hat." I already knew that, but I did my best not to look exasperated. "How about a hundred dollars?"

"Sir"—if he was going to *ma'am* me, well then, I had to *sir* him—"I'm sorry. I can't sell it." At this point, it felt more like a matter of principle. How could I sell something that had been given by a friend, that had been picked out especially for me (even if that suddenly seemed a little insulting)? How could I make a profit on such an article, an item that couldn't have cost more than a few dollars, an item that announced so loudly that such value as it had had nothing to do with money? It just wasn't right.

"He *really* likes it." I glanced over at the bar. The really big older dude was still not cracking a smile.

"Can I think about it?" I asked. I couldn't just cave. Was this a joke? Were they just messing with me? I wondered if it had become a matter of principle for both parties. He returned to his gang, looking forlorn and dejected. He had failed.

"Oh, come on, just take the money," Owen said. "His friend likes the hat more than you do. And besides, it's hideous. Personally, I never want to see it again."

But this wasn't about aesthetics. And they were still looking in my direction. Most of my friends had ceased to pay the goings-on any attention by this point. But I was mulling over a strategy. Owen was right: It was an ugly and unbecoming hat. What exactly a big old biker wanted it for was beyond me. Maybe it reminded him of someone, or of some better time in his life, maybe back in the seventies, when presumably everyone, even bikers, wore dumb rainbow-colored chapeaux, when, maybe, he'd gotten his first bike and first set out on the back roads of America, *Easy Rider*-style. Or maybe there was something deeper behind this pursuit, a real tragedy: recollections of a deceased beloved who'd once had in her possession a similar hat and then, when they were touring cross-country—maybe on their honeymoon, even—she collided with a discarded beer can in the middle of the road, shot up into the air, and went tumbling to her premature death, the hat tucked under her helmet, but given the terrible extent of her injuries, irretrievable?

Or maybe his mother, who raised him up to be something more than he was, who had *tried*, just like in the Merle Haggard song, had been a knitter.

Maybe he just liked the thing.

And maybe it was the number of beers I'd drunk by then that made me see the situation differently. If he *was* just fucking with me, he was doing it with admirable, dogged tenacity, never once raising his voice, never being anything but utterly polite and calm. The thing was hideous. And my friend, who'd given it to me, well, she was a biker herself—not a lifer like these guys, but an enthusiast, anyway—so she'd not only understand why I'd let the thing go, she'd be happy about it, maybe even proud. And as for the northern weather being cold, that particular night demanded nothing more than a quick dash from bar to car and car to door. I'd survive. There was more than one hat in the world.

I felt bolder. I took the hat off, gripped it in one hand and my beer in the other, and walked up to the biker. "All right," I said. "It's all yours. I mean, it's your friend's."

He looked like he might cry. "So," he asked, getting back down to business, "how much you want?"

"I can't take your money for it," I said. "But if you want to buy a round for my friends and me, that would be nice."

"It's a deal," he said. "Ma'am, I can't thank you enough."

And that's when I knew that whatever else this had been

about, it wasn't just a joke after all. It meant *something*, even if I'd never know what. All I did know was that this man loved that other man—as leader, brother, lover, who knew?—and was determined to give him this gift. He put energy into it, and emotion, and I was moved, too. "Sir, you're welcome."

There was a loud clinking of glasses and bottles among the bikers. The guy who'd led the negotiations victoriously crowned his buddy with the hat, making him king of whatever ragged brotherhood this was, and the whole gang of these previously stern, stone-faced men was smiling and laughing, a bunch of kids, a bunch of little boys. A round soon appeared at my table, my friends and I drank up, celebrated this curious coronation, and lit back out on Route 7 and into Vermont, where it became Route 9, where late at night you could not see the lush loping valley that opened out into a great bowl just off to the right as soon as you crossed the border, but you knew it was there, and you could feel it, even in the dark, all that space, all that green country and sweet air.

When people asked me what had become of that hat—its disappearance would not go unnoticed—I could now tell them that it had fallen into the grateful hands of its true and rightful owner, and was off with him on an adventure somewhere. And every subsequent visit to the Man of Kent held out the possibility that something a little magical might happen, even if it was just a conversation with John, or the first cheeseburger I bit into after seven years of vegetarianism, or just the simple pleasure of introducing someone who'd never been there before to this place, this special place where a chicken might wander in at any moment, where surprised English tourists might pop in and be startled at first by this more-than-the-real-thing, more-English-than-the-English but still very upstate New York simulacrum of something so familiar to them, where the respect of a good barman made at least one college girl feel like a citizen of the world. As long as I had a willing and sober-enough friend to drive and enough cash for a round, there was no place I'd rather be, even if I could only get there once every few weeks or, sadly, even less often.

But the rarity of my visits made the place all the more alluring, a destination, not a default. When I needed to be there, I really needed to be there. And never did I need to be there more than the night after my college graduation. All I knew for sure was that I'd spend that summer in Vermont, before getting on with the rest of my life, before entering the real world, whatever that might be. My friend Theo, who had so often been the designated driver to the Man of Kent, had graduated the year before me, but he'd come up that week-end to see his friends get their diplomas and to come to our senior party. It had been a busy, weird weekend: The pres-ence of my always-unpredictable mother made me nervous. At dinner the night before graduation, her then-boyfriend

had a pain in his chest and started to kvetch, loudly. He
didn't have a heart attack, but it seemed possible. My brother
was returning from a few weeks of work in France, where
he'd gotten mysteriously and seriously ill. And as for me,
well, I realized that no matter how much I'd complained
about college, how many times I had considered dropping
out as I had in high school, when it was all winding down, I
understood that it had been the life. I had come to love the
small town of North Bennington, where I had lived in comfortable pseudo-independence for two years. I loved the bar
just a block up the street, where I spent nearly every night in
the company of a few friends and professors and locals. Reading poetry and philosophy as though it were my job, thinking
about Yeats and Tolstoy and Joyce and Kant, was not such a
bad way to keep oneself occupied. I had become known as a
political agitator on campus, as a poet, as a girl who could
hold her liquor and still get things done. And now that it was
over, I knew I'd never have it so easy again.

Ma and her boyfriend and my brother cleared out after
brunch the morning after graduation. I went back to my
apartment, where I'd let a bunch of students crash who'd
been kicked out of their dorms now that the semester had
ended. Their stuff was everywhere: suitcases and backpacks
and duffel bags in my living room, contact lens solution next
to my bathroom sink. But they were all out doing something.
I sat alone all afternoon in my cluttered living room, flipped
through my senior thesis, a project I'd spent the good part of

the year writing, and it reminded me of how lucky I'd been those last four years. The young have a talent for magnifying everything, especially everything bad: every little failure, every heartache, every shitty day, every little test of one's character, every disappointment, becomes so huge. And all your Blake and Brecht and Orwell, all your deep-seated life-long class consciousness, all your cloistered political agitating, everything you may have read, or believed, or done, did little to stop this, little to say, *Don't you see how good you've got it?* It felt weak and silly and self-indulgent to feel so sorry for myself, but there I was. Later, Theo showed up at my door and found me crying at my desk. He didn't have to ask what was wrong; he'd gone through the thing just a year earlier.

"I'm sorry you're sad," he said. "I wish I could do something for you."

I shook my head. "Thanks. I'll be okay." I was glad Theo had shown up, but I couldn't think of anything he could do to make me feel better, less afraid, comforted.

"Wanna go to the Man of Kent?"

He asked exactly the right question. If anything might console me, an evening at the Man of Kent was it.

Off we went, just before the sun set, out on that curvy country road, past the great green bowl of the valley, past the reservoir, listening to the Minutemen on the car stereo in his white egglike little Honda. I felt totally enclosed, in a good way, and grateful for my friend, who had intuited exactly what I needed. By then, Theo was no longer straight-edge—

he'd capitulated to the pleasures of drink in his senior year—
but I knew that he knew that this evening, this trip to the
bar, was for me, not for him, that he would let me get as drunk
as I needed, as drunk as I wanted to, and he would shepherd
me safely home. "Hello, darling!" John greeted me when we
walked in. "How are you?"

"I just graduated, John," I said.

"Well done," he said. "So you're leaving us, then?"

"I guess so," I said. "After the summer."

"Well, you'll be back. I know you will."

Would I? I hoped so. I knew I couldn't stay in that part of
the world forever, though it was tempting. He gave me a Belgian cherry lambic on the house. Theo and I took a table and
talked. I thanked him for taking me there. We toasted each
other.

And I didn't really get drunk at all, not on booze, anyway.
Instead, I slowly drank my Belgian beers and got drunk on
the bar itself. I thought about everything that had made the
Man of Kent possible—thank God John had somehow settled in this little community in a picturesque but unglamor-
ous corner of upstate New York. His bar had been a blessing
to me, a secret garden—and the gentlest, warmest place to
observe, learn, and enact a transition from youth to adulthood, to study and appreciate a bar's unwritten but powerful
code of honor. Be good to the people serving you drinks; be
open to your fellow patrons, no matter how different they are
from you. Gently mind the people you bring with you, but

have authority. Have fun, but not at the expense of anyone else's fun. A bar is never yours alone.

Sitting there that night, all the songs John played, all the memorabilia, the bar towels and cricket bats and jerseys and accoutrements, all these things that had initially just looked like so much kitsch took on richer properties: This bar was a labor of love, a pouring-forth of someone's heart, someone from far away, someone who'd lived in many places and, it seemed, lived many lives. Every item represented a choice or a gift; everything was about John, and about that some-times incoherent mix of customers, the patrons he protected, served, nurtured, cared for.

Before Theo and I left that night, I made sure to tell John how much the place had meant to me, how much I loved every visit I'd made there. "Well, you've been one of our favorites, too," he said. And maybe he said that to everybody, but I liked to believe it was true. I'd never exactly been a regular there—its distance made that impossible. But even if I didn't know everybody as soon as I walked in, I knew they were all okay; they loved this bar, they got it, and that was enough.

In the summer of 2007, my husband and I went to Vermont. On the way back to New York, we stopped at the Man of Kent. I couldn't imagine not stopping by when I was in the

area, but it was especially good that we paid that particular
visit. We sat down at the bar, happy to find John behind it.
After a few minutes of catching up, John dropped a bomb:
he told us that he'd sold the bar. He still might tend bar
sometimes, he told us, but this was it.

I couldn't believe it, but he was getting older, spending
more time away, gearing up to retire. I didn't want to give
him the third degree about the new owner. But I did have
questions.

"I think they'll keep the place pretty much as it is," he
told me, but that wasn't completely reassuring. I couldn't
stand the thought of one single bar towel out of place. It was
perfect—too-bright lighting and all—and I've never been a
believer in change for change's sake. I certainly couldn't
imagine anyone improving on the place.

There are so many bars where the owners are invisible,
where they just fade into the background, collect the cash,
sign the checks, take care of the payroll, maybe stop in to
make sure the place is busy, but don't really get involved. For
owners like that, it's a business—they might as well be selling
auto parts or groceries or pet supplies. They are effectively
anonymous—Oz-like, machinating behind the scenes, but
not out among the men and women whose patronage is their
livelihood. And for certain bars, that's fine. But the Man of
Kent was not that kind of bar; it was exactly the opposite. Its
owner's life and history, interests and tastes, animated the

whole place. The Man of Kent was an extension of John, an extension of his home—the one right next door, and the one across the Atlantic.

A more recent visit eased my mind: The place is still thriving, the bar towels are still there, the Piaf songs still playing. The new owner gets it. Bikers are still staring down college students, farmers still arguing politics with professors. And best of all, John is still there, no longer the owner, but behind the bar during the early weekday shift. It has managed to retain its spirit, its singular genius loci. It's still there, still set back on that green stretch of roadside, awaiting any pilgrims who might find their way there to take their drink and sweet rest. And maybe, if they're as young as I was when I first stepped foot in the Man of Kent, they'll also learn a thing or two about how to be a good bar patron, as I did. The Man of Kent was always farther away than I wanted it to be, even when it was only a matter of ten miles or so. Now it is hundreds of miles away. But it still comforts me to think about it, and about the gently pastoral—admittedly romanticized—life it represents. Now it feels like it exists in a parallel world, still there, if impossibly beyond my physical reach, but rooted deeply in this drinker's heart.

6.

LATE TO THE PARTY

Puffy's Tavern, New York City

One early autumn evening in 1995, Puffy's Tavern appeared before me like a shimmering urban mirage, like a dream bar vision out of an Edward Hopper painting, anchoring its corner of Hudson and Harrison Streets in TriBeCa in stalwart brick and great plate glass windows. Some nights, Puffy's felt like the saddest damn song Tom Waits ever sang; others, it was vibrant and alive, humming with conversation and cosmopolitan good cheer. Puffy's was scuffed black-and-white tile, barroom green walls gone grayish with ash and age, a battle-ravaged dartboard, sad-faced drunks, and regulars ready with stories to tell— whether you felt like listening or not. And more often than not, I did.

Puffy's was beautiful. In its way. Like an old weather-beaten chanteuse with running mascara who still manages to break your heart as soon as she starts singing. But ask, and anyone will tell you that Puffy's is not what it used to be. Then again, TriBeCa isn't what it used to be, either. And to be fair, by the time I showed up there, both the neighborhood and the bar *already* weren't what they used to be—though they've drifted still further from their former selves in the years since.

Puffy's, in a sense, predates "TriBeCa"; that graceless tripartite designation was, by most accounts, imposed upon the area by realtors when the neighborhood was just waking up—with a hangover—after well over a decade as a sparsely populated artists' enclave, where pioneers had staked their territorial claims and carved spaces first and foremost for painting and printing and sculpting, and only incidentally for living, out of drafty old loft buildings on badly lit cobbled streets. In those days, "TriBeCa" didn't exist; the neighborhood was just downtown, or the Lower West Side (as one friend, who could never quite stomach the new name, still insists on calling it), or where you found yourself when you got off the IRT 1 train at Franklin Street, or the express at Chambers Street—the seedy two-way artery at its southern edge—or if you strayed too far west from the courts after a day of jury duty or from dinner in Chinatown. By the mid 1990s, TriBeCa was on its way to becoming the wealthiest neighborhood per capita in Manhattan, outdoing even the western flank of the Upper East Side. Artists had cleaned up the area, made it habitable, vibrant—and desirable. The thankless result was that bankers and movie stars and others from the ranks of the superrich would, within a generation, swoop in to displace them. In New York City, of

course, the rich have always been with us, and they have
effectively taken over: the teachers and social workers and
struggling artists and writers and performers who populated
the city of my youth can no longer afford Manhattan. On this
small island, less and less space is available to those who
were, and are, responsible for so much of its identity and
spirit.

The first time I drank at Puffy's, it was with college
friends; we'd all recently graduated. We claimed the far end
of the uncomfortable painted wooden banquette that lines
the wall opposite the long, dark, imposing bar. *Banquette* is
euphemistic; it's a bench, really, likely slapped together with
plywood and two-by-fours, God knows when. We got there
late one afternoon—a Saturday, probably—and stayed well
into the early morning hours. The bartender—an earthy,
vivacious woman in her forties, a rarity in New York City
bars—held court, expertly mixing cocktails and drawing
pints, dancing energetically to "Brick House" or some other
loud beat-heavy number issuing from the gorgeous old jukebox while making everyone feel welcome (*loved*, even) all at
once. I liked the place. In fact, I felt pretty sure I might be
falling in love with it. I made a few return visits with friends,
but I had the sense that I belonged there solo. I had never
before felt so territorial about a bar, for mysterious reasons.

In September 1995, I was in graduate school, working on
a doctorate in English literature, and not long after my first
night at Puffy's I started teaching freshman English at the

huge community college just a block west of the bar. The Borough of Manhattan Community College has about a million students—I am only exaggerating a little—and like many campuses of its early 1970s vintage, it was designed with specs better suited to a correctional facility than to a university. Drive past it on the West Side Highway and, with its sparse, horizontal windows looking out at the Hudson River like suspicious squinting eyes and its pitiless stretches of drab brick, it looks like a prison.

The campus came into being in the years after four students were murdered at Kent State, after Mark Rudd took Low Memorial Library at Columbia hostage, after student activists tore shit up all over the country. By design, BMCC has no quad, no central space where students can congregate—or protest. The sheer physical hardness of the campus is oppressive. But I liked teaching. I liked my students, who seemed to come from everywhere: Haiti and Poland, Russia and Macao, Serbia and the Dominican Republic and Greece and Ivory Coast and Staten Island. The range of ability and talent matched the international diversity; there were some brilliant people in those classrooms and some insufferable dumbasses. But they were never boring, and I took to teaching pretty quickly and easily. Still, as much as I enjoyed teaching at BMCC, my affection for it abruptly deteriorated outside of the classroom. My office, for instance, was shared with some fifty other underpaid and often embittered adjunct professors of English.

I was living just across town, near the South Street Seaport, in a boxy, dark, charmless apartment with gray industrial carpeting and low drop ceilings. My roommate was a friend from college—a smart, sad Goth with jet-black hair that cascaded nearly to her ass and a constellation of deathy tattoos sprayed about her pale body. Though we had been close as undergraduates, Vanessa and I turned out to be a bad match as living companions. Her Gothic mien was more than subcultural affect; it was deep and hard-earned. She'd lived through personal tragedy that few people at her young age had had to endure, and seemed, at least back then, to carry the heavy weight of loss with her at all times. By comparison, my own sadnesses seemed slight, but they were there nonetheless. Grad school wasn't working out for me. At my tiny college in Vermont, for better or worse, it had been easy to stand out and to be spoiled by the attention—friendship, even—of my professors. At a big school in the big city, I was doing nothing to distinguish myself, and at the same time I had little but contempt for the great majority of my fellow students. In a seminar on the Romantics, when we were discussing Mary Shelley's *Frankenstein*, I made what seemed to me a winning, if obvious, joke. The first time someone in the room spoke the book's title aloud, I corrected him. "*Fronkensteen*," I insisted. Either no one in the class had seen Mel Brooks's masterpiece *Young Frankenstein*—which seemed to me not merely impossible, but downright tragic—or they pretended they hadn't. In either case, it felt like one more little depressing moment in a year that was quickly filling up with them. The gloom of my apartment, whose few windows faced only the back sides of other buildings—hardly brightened by my roommate's poster collection (heavy on the Cure) and Sisters of Mercy–centric sound track—only made it worse. The place confirmed my unhappiness and my nagging, if premature, sense of failure. I called it Bleak House.

Puffy's, for all its louche allure, was the perfect antidote to graduate school, to my work environment, and to my housing situation. For a time, I'd go in the afternoons after teaching, return to that little stretch of banquette near the back corner, and quietly grade papers. The afternoon bartender at the time was Louie, a flirtatious painter in his fifties with an abundant head of salt-and-pepper hair, a dense mustache that would not have been out of place on the sepia-photographed countenance of a Union soldier in 1863, and a wardrobe of homespun shirts with wooden buttons, suspenders, and breeches. The first time I met him I was in a foul mood and ordered a pint of Guinness and a Jameson, neat. He smiled slyly. "Girl," he asked me, not exactly rhetorically, "where you been all my life?"

Most afternoons I'd stick to Guinness, keep to myself, and slog through a tower of freshman essays. But I eavesdropped shamelessly on the conversations among the guys at the bar. It was never anything scandalous: neighborhood news and a smattering of gossip, pretty standard among people who'd known one another seemingly forever. But they were an animated bunch. Bill was a sandpaper-voiced ironworker who'd spent years working on the Manhattan Bridge and had a nose that looked like it had seen more than its share of fights and occupational hazards. He usually had a Yorkshire terrier in tow, wearing a little satin bow in her silky topknot. *"Emma,"* he'd coo at her with gravelly affection, stroking her head and chin. The dog was named after Emma Goldman. Emma was not the only canine in the crowd: Henry, an aging overweight beagle, usually accompanied Walker, a homeless man known to just about everyone in the neighborhood, loved by some, tolerated by others. Probably in his fifties at the time, he reputedly spoke about a dozen (mainly classical) languages and had been a tournament Scrabble champion. Anyone who tried to talk to Walker about the shelter system or encourage him to "get help" was instantly rebuffed. Even I, the queen of the bleeding hearts, who badly wished to regard myself as a helper of humankind and a friend particularly to people who were poor, marginalized, and outcast, knew better than to dare. He made it perfectly clear that he was more than smart enough to seek help and make use of whatever resources existed; he happened to prefer his life the way it was, thank you very much. Walking Henry, who belonged to a friend, seemed to provide Walker with enough money to feed himself and buy the occasional drink. I also got used to the sight of a wiry guy named Ken, a bundle of nervous human energy, who'd stop by, chat with Louie, maybe have a drink, maybe not, and disappear as quickly as

he'd arrived. Within a month or so, I'd be working side by
side with Ken on the little magazine of literature and art he'd
been putting out since 1971, the year I was born.

Everything felt right to me at Puffy's: the look of the
place, its tone and cadences, the absence of a television, the
presence of the old jukebox loaded with classic rock 'n' roll
45s ("Satisfaction," "Runaround Sue") and some curiosities
(like Randy Newman's "Short People"), the playing card—a
six of hearts—confoundingly affixed to the high ceiling in
the front right corner (lodged there, I am told, by a long-ago
bartender/magician who liked to entertain his drunks with
card tricks). It was comforting and reassuring; it was not
home and not school and not the office. The afternoon guys
were welcoming and friendly, but politely left me to my
Guinness and my work. Then, having finished grading, cri-
tiquing, and often despairing over a substantial-enough number of papers, I might reward myself in the early evening
with a nice Jameson on the rocks.

For that reward, I would move from the back bench to a
barstool up in the front corner. And that was probably the
single most important development in my drinking life. I
became a regular, a person who belonged to a bar, and to
whom a bar belonged. I understood that though I loved the
bars I patronized in college, I was only passing through; four
years and I'd be gone. But I had, at the time, no desire ever to
leave New York again. So why would I ever leave Puffy's—
this perfect, picturesque, comfortable spot?

I found myself staying later and later, watching the early evening crowd replace the afternoon crowd, watching one bartender relieve another as the former counted out the till and tallied up his or her tips, then switched over to the civilian side of the bar for a very welcome post-shift drink. Evening, and the locals, the ones whose jobs made day drinking impossible, filed in. Like the afternoon crowd, most of them were nearly a generation older than me. The really, really tall guy. The ponytailed Southern one with the anxiety and the twang. The cowboy, outfitted more appropriately for a day out on the range than on the streets of the great metropolis. The blond guy with the boyish face and the interest in post-structuralist philosophers. They were so at ease with one another, so familiar. They'd bullshit and laugh, and I'd sit a few stools down and listen. They were mostly guys, yes, but there were a few women, too. The one with dark curls and sparkly blue eyes and a great love of beer. The foxy, witty one with a little gravel in her voice; she'd graduated from Bennington in 1969, back when it was *really* cool. The sad, sweet one who slurred her words as she sat below the portrait of her deceased beloved.

Aside from the bartenders, I don't know who talked to me first. Not the cowboy. Not the Southerner. Not the boyish one. It might have been Sonia, with the curls. Or maybe it was Jimmy, the tall guy, who had a deep tall-guy voice and a long face and glasses, and a distinct sweetness about him that was matched by an equally unmistakable watchfulness. He knew everyone there. He knew their stories, their wives, their habits, their histories. And through all the years of drinking together, I sensed that he was the one who remembered, and recorded, what they'd experienced in one another's company. So many of Puffy's conversations, especially among the guys, started with, "Hey, remember that time . . . ?" And, of course, I did *not* remember that time—that time when everyone was dancing on the tabletops, that time when so-and-so disarmed a mugger in the shady little alley behind the bar with his blunt assertion that, really, his day couldn't get any worse anyway, that time when . . . that time when . . . But I was happy just to take it in, to listen, to imagine what a past here, a history here, felt like.

But certainly it was Will, the boyish blond, with whom I had my first substantial Puffy's conversation—fun and lively and *long*—and with whom I felt an instant kindred-spirit connection. I got Will, and he—this funny, smart, deeply charming person—got me.

At the time, I was all too eager to tell people that I considered myself a Muggletonian. Muggletonians were a radical Protestant dissenting sect of the seventeenth century, and the great historian E. P. Thompson argued that William Blake's mother might have been one. The Blake connection alone might have been enough for me. But there was more: Instead of worshipping in churches, which they considered pointless and hierarchical, the Muggletonians instead are said to have "worshipped" in taverns, going from public house to public

house praying and singing and making political trouble—
and drinking. I'd first heard about them in college, when one
of my professors ID'd me as a Muggletonian. I could see his
point, so I readily claimed Muggletonianism as my true faith
and happily preached its dissenter doctrines to anyone who'd
listen. At Puffy's, people were ready to be converted.

Will was more than a skillful conversationalist. He was
an intellectual and a lover of history. He'd spent a lot of time
in the former Czechoslovakia and, although a nonbeliever
himself, he felt an affinity for the Hussites—the Bohemian
followers of Jan Hus, who was burned for heresy in 1415. We
must have talked dissenting Christians and poetry and politics until three or four in the morning, with some of the other
regulars occasionally contributing their two cents, or making
fun of the highfalutin and vaguely religious content of our
conversation.

Although Will had been drinking at Puffy's since the seventies, he wasn't blasé about it. He knew that here, here, we
had something rare and special. "Café society," he said with a
sigh, and we clinked glasses. And at its best, that's exactly
what Puffy's was: a distinctly American, distinctly New York
version of European café society, replete with thick smoke
and friendly argument and laughter. Where else could two
drunks talk fervently about early modern religious movements, and politics and life, and God knows what else, all
night, laughing, occasionally shouting, having a ridiculously
good time? Until then, I hadn't found it—at least not since

Dublin. From then on, the tall one—Jimmy—frequently announced, in his booming voice, "It's the Muggletonian!" on my arrival at the bar. Jimmy and Will had lived in the neighborhood since the mid-1970s and had been friends since they were in their twenties.

Very soon, they were my friends, too. There was no hazing period at Puffy's. I fit in right away, although, in one significant way, I was not like them: Like many of the other regulars, Will and Jimmy were painters. The place was crawling with artists—even among the bartenders. Some of them had done well for themselves in the previous decade's art boom. Some had managed to hold on to at least some of the money, some of the success they'd earned. Some had lived it up and partied like crazy and lost it all. Most were somewhere in between, still painting, still showing their work, but doing construction, proofreading, anything to stay afloat. What made Puffy's so inviting, what made it work so well, was that here the painters and poets and designers and ironworkers and occasional academics and even lawyers all found common ground.

The days of abstract expressionist heavyweights like de Kooning and Pollock and Rothko holding court at the Cedar Tavern were long gone, but this had to be the next best thing. I was twenty-four at the time and holding my own just fine with these fortysomethings. At least I could teach them something about Muggletonians. Because, for me, Puffy's was itself a classroom—a protracted, whiskey-soaked lesson in art history and New York culture, a repository of downtown lore and legend. I cared about politics. Hey, I cared about art. I had grown up in New York, going to museums and galleries and theater and concerts. Maybe the problem was that I'd taken all that for granted. In college, so many of my friends were painters and sculptors. But at Puffy's, even though I could match those art guys drink for drink, I quickly discovered—to my mild horror—that I *did not get all the references.*

One night pretty early on in my time there, the guys were talking about something—God knows what—and laughing. "Like a Robert Ryman painting" was the punch line. Robert Ryman. *Who?* I quietly cursed myself for not having taken any art history classes. But even as my ignorance embarrassed me, I was excited that here, among these painters, these drinkers, these talkers, I stood to learn so much. When Cory, the Southern painter, rhapsodized about Albert Pinkham Ryder, about his risky technical experiments and abiding Romanticism, I made it my business to find out who the hell this person was, and he soon became one of my favorite painters, too.

Ken, the wiry, intense guy I'd often spotted in the afternoons, also came around in the evenings now and then, and we got to talking, too. He was a poet and the publisher of a cultish little magazine of literature and art. He had interviewed Auden and Ginsberg and Creeley, spent time in the company of Bukowski, been conned by Corso. And even though I made it clear that I'd rather be reading Blake or Yeats or Wordsworth over any of them any day, I was impressed. His intelligence was swift and sharp; maybe because I knew he was, or had anyway been raised, Catholic, it struck me as Jesuitical.

"Young poets in New York write about art," he told me, as though it were a given. I gave it a shot. But my experiences at Puffy's with the art guys had shown me that I didn't know nearly as much about art as I thought I did. Ken recommended books, including Robert Atkins's extremely handy *ArtSpeak*, an overview of art movements and ideas. I'd sit up at night reading it, absorbing as much information as I was able, so that I could better follow whatever the hell my Puffy's friends were talking about, that I might know my Art Brut from my Arte Povera, my new realism from my photorealism. (Robert Ryman: Minimalist. White paintings. Check.) One evening at Puffy's, Ken nodded in the direction of a glamorous older woman who looked European, or South American, or both. Her bearing was regal, if not downright imperious. I'd seen her before. She usually drank sake and kept to herself. "You know who she is?" I did not.

"Marisol," he said. One of the most celebrated living women in the visual arts. I clearly knew nothing. Marisol often had two imposing dogs in tow. One was known to be good-natured; the other, vicious. She generally paid me no mind, but on one occasion she moved from one end of the bar down to the front corner, where I had planted myself for the previous few hours. "I have to talk to you," she said conspiratorially in her high and heavily accented voice. "You zee zat repulsive man?" She gestured toward the back of the room at a burly disheveled character. "He wants to sleep with me. Zo I *must* talk to *you* eenstead." Not exactly a compliment, but I was glad to be of service.

Not long after I'd learned who Marisol was, I showed up at Puffy's one evening, surprised and saddened to discover that a memorial service for one of her dogs (the good one) was in full swing. When I walked in, someone was eloquently eulogizing the dead Akita. I nudged a friend's elbow and whispered, "He's good."

"I think it's Edward Albee," she said, sotto voce.

The next day I told my father—a notorious and enthusiastic name-dropper who could seldom be one-upped—that at my bar the previous night, I'd heard Edward Albee eulogize this artist named Marisol's dog. His eyes got huge. "Do you have any idea what a big deal she was in the sixties?" By then, I had some idea. "I saw her at a party once. She was stunningly beautiful. Sinatra was also there," he said. "And I couldn't decide who was more famous."

I hardly socialized with my fellow students. Why would I, when I had these friends at Puffy's, who, I was sure, were giving me a more valuable education anyway? Jimmy's stories about traveling the world with the famous painter he worked for were certainly more interesting than anything in my dry American literature seminar. The collective reminiscences of seeing bands like the Talking Heads and Blondie and the New York Dolls at places like Max's Kansas City and CBGB, the all-night benders at Tyrannosaurus Rex, the openings at Mary Boone and parties with Jasper Johns were riveting. I might have been the only native New Yorker in the bunch, but my new friends had lived in a New York I'd never really known, a New York that was louder and dirtier and sexier and infinitely more interesting than the one I'd grown up in.

I not only felt understood at Puffy's, I felt valued. Moreover, I even felt pretty. Some women walk into bars and heads turn instantly. Everybody knows this. I am not one of those women. I've always been a big girl, which, without going into the complicated, fraught cultural politics of weight, always seemed to give me a literal kind of buffer in bar culture and made it possible to be accepted among men without inevitably becoming the object of romantic attention. But at Puffy's, my friends were frequently telling me I was *beautiful*. Was it something in the water? Or maybe the lighting? Was it because they were artists and saw things, and people, differently? It made me feel good. So good that I started to believe them, that when I looked into the mirror in the teeny tiny bathroom at the back of the bar to the right of the dartboard, well, I thought I looked pretty good, too. There was no shortage of sociable and largely harmless flirting among the regulars, and I happily participated. I became bold enough to flirt with non-regulars, too. And, from time to time, after a few drinks, after the talk and flirtation, I became bold enough to go home with near- or total strangers. Despite the risks, that, too, seemed better than another night at Bleak House.

Within months, Puffy's had overtaken every aspect of my life. Grad school was pretty much a bust. I fell behind with all of my schoolwork. I'd signed on with Ken as assistant editor of his magazine; my responsibilities included brandishing a hockey stick in his direction when he wasn't working hard enough (he's Canadian, so it made a perfect kind of sense), for which I was "paid" in lunches at the local sports bar or at the café at the other end of Harrison Street and drinks at Puffy's. We'd cut and paste, old-school style, and talk poetry and art. I celebrated my twenty-fifth birthday with dinner at an Italian restaurant with Sonia and some of the other women among the Puffy's regulars. Once, when Louie the bartender was in a bind, I agreed to pick his kids up from school. I'd even invited Paul—the extremely bright Irish bartender—to come talk to my class at BMCC about Irish culture and politics when I'd assigned a few stories from Joyce's *Dubliners*. It's not that Paul wasn't qualified—he was a native Dubliner, a Trinity alum, and a natural teacher—but was it, possibly, just kind of weird to invite your Thursday night bartender to come and lecture to your Monday afternoon class?

Maybe this was not a normal way for a twenty-five-year-old woman to live her life. Maybe something really *was* wrong with me.

But at least at Puffy's, most of the time, everything felt

easy and good. This was not the case at school, where I was seriously fucking up. Or with my family, from whom I felt more alienated than ever—with the exception of my maternal grandmother, whom I visited every Sunday afternoon, normally bleary-eyed after a long night at the bar, not that she noticed. It was certainly not the case at home, where I proved to be a shitty and irresponsible roommate, seldom present, frequently late with the rent and other bills. The friendship I'd once enjoyed with my roommate had almost dissolved completely, and I knew it was my fault. I was living my life, and my life took place in a bar—a bar from which I'd just as soon have my old friends stay away, even the ones I used to go to bars with and drink with all the time.

Vanessa was a devoted journal-keeper; she'd kept journals forever, probably since she'd learned to write. And she was in the habit of leaving her journal, an oversize hardback black book, splayed open on the little table just beyond our tiny kitchen. This, I told myself, surely meant that she *wanted* me to read it. In my heart, I knew it was wrong to read someone's diary, even if they left it *wide open on a table you shared.* Oh, it was wrong. Wrong wrong wrong. And I found it totally irresistible.

One morning, as I'm sitting at that little table, drinking my coffee, smoking a cig, slightly hungover as usual, I see the journal in front of me. Open. And the first thing that catches my eye is my name. There. In black ink, in my roommate's distinctive, cramped, jagged, anxious hand. I can't say exactly what she'd written verbatim. But I do recall that she observed, not surprisingly, what a fuckup I was in so many ways. I was aware that this was not an unreasonable assessment. She opined further that I was not, however, a terrible person. That I was, actually, a pretty nice person. *Well, that's nice.* Even really mean people, she continued, are nice when they're around me. I wasn't sure who these mean people she had in mind were, but I liked this fine, too. She remarked that for as long as we'd known each other, I'd demonstrated a knack for making myself "indispensable" at bars; she'd seen it in college at the bar in North Bennington, and to a lesser degree at the Man of Kent, and she could tell that it had happened at Puffy's, too. *Indispensable.* An interesting way of putting it, I thought, but sure, fine. All I ever seemed to do these days was go to the bar, she noted. *Well, you've got me there.* I couldn't argue with her on that point.

And one more thing.

She wrote, *Rosie has a serious alcohol problem.* Or something like that. Maybe it was even starker. Maybe it was *Rosie is an alcoholic.* Or even *Rosie is a serious alcoholic.* I managed not to spit-take my coffee across the page.

I could live with being a fuckup. I had lived with being one for most of my life. I thought that when I finished college, I was on the right track. I'd had setbacks since graduating, but surely they would pass. And, for now, I could also live with being a disappointment. I was still young, and there was hope that someday I would redeem myself. I was sort of flattered by the "indispensable" bit, and accepted it as a peculiar but not necessarily bad trait. But I wasn't so comfortable with the realization that Vanessa—someone I knew well, who knew me well, someone who was no lightweight when it came to the drink herself—considered me an alcoholic. Because—dumbly or blindly, maybe disclosing some real deficit in the self-reflection department—no matter how much I drank, no matter how many hours I'd logged sitting on my ass on a barstool in the front corner of Puffy's Tavern, the thought had never occurred to me. Not once.

Maybe something really *was* wrong with me.

What did it mean to be an alcoholic, anyway? To my knowledge, there was no precedent among my kin. My mother, fond of the occasional whiskey sour (on the sweet side, preferably) or Bloody Mary or screwdriver, was never a champ in the booze department. After two drinks, three tops, she was reliably buzzed and content to go no further. I think I'd seen her drunk, properly drunk, once, during a party she'd thrown for a friend when I was about ten. My father's drinking habits were pretty tame, too. No, I knew of no relative with a reputation for being a serious boozer, no hardcore *shikker* among the Schaaps.

But I did have one reference point for what an alcoholic was: a close friend of my mother's, with whom I'd spent a lot of time when I was growing up. Angie always had a huge bottle of cheap gin stashed in the giant satchel she lugged around. I couldn't remember a time I didn't smell alcohol

on her breath, a time she wasn't drunk. I knew I wasn't like
that, like her. I drank in bars, not at home. I drank because I
like being in bars, and that's what you did there. You drank.
And you talked. But it could not be denied that I was spending an awful lot of my time in bars. Drinking.

The National Institute on Alcohol Abuse and Alcoholism
of the National Institutes of Health tells us that alcoholism is
a disease characterized by the following four symptoms:

> *Craving:* A strong need, or urge, to drink.
> *Loss of control:* Not being able to stop drinking once
> drinking has begun.
> *Physical dependence:* Withdrawal symptoms, such as
> nausea, sweating, shakiness, and anxiety after
> stopping drinking.
> *Tolerance:* The need to drink greater amounts of
> alcohol to get "high."

I considered the facts. Yes, I was drinking almost every
night. How much? Hard to say. I hadn't been counting. The
liquor flowed freely at Puffy's. The buybacks were bountiful.
Did I crave alcohol? No. I loved drinking, but more than
anything, I craved the bar, not the booze, though of course
they went together. Did I lose control? Ever since I'd blacked
out as a teenager in California, I did not want to drink
expressly to get drunk—though inevitably I sometimes did
get drunk. I drank to feel more relaxed, certainly, but not to

get wasted, and not nonstop. Did it take a lot for me to get a good buzz? It is probably true that my tolerance was peaking just around that time—I could hold quite a lot of whiskey in my twenties—but even after just a few sips of Jameson I could feel its calming and comforting effects. And yes, I was able to stop—as soon as I left the bar.

And *that* was the hard part: leaving. I frequently stayed at Puffy's for hours and hours—marathon stretches that lasted from late afternoon until early morning. I thought back on the many long nights I'd spent there. I'd been having fun, hadn't I? Yes, I had. I'd met interesting, smart people who, in a real and undidactic way, had taught me so much. What had I been doing? Well, mostly, I drank and talked and listened and made friends. Was that so bad? No, I decided, it wasn't *so* bad.

But. But. But. There were a few nights that, on reflection, troubled me. I rarely stayed late enough to close the place, but I recall one time when I did. After four—when bars in New York are supposed to pack it in—the closing bartender dimmed the lights in the front and the few regulars who remained there moved to the back. I stepped out of Puffy's in broad daylight (it was probably nearly seven A.M.) and made my way two blocks north to Socrates, the local coffee shop. I downed a few cups of coffee and had a greasy, delicious bacon sandwich. In the ladies' room, I splashed my face with water. And then I walked back past Puffy's—finally shut-

tered until the afternoon shift—to BMCC, where I had an
eight-thirty A.M. Intro to English Literature class to teach. All
the coffee and bacon in the world really couldn't counteract
the plain truth that I was still drunk. Would my students
notice? Probably. *I* always did when, in college, a couple of
my own professors occasionally taught under the influence—
not that I held it against them. Worse: Would they notice I
was wearing exactly what I'd worn yesterday? Some would.
For sure. In my office I gave myself something between a pep
talk and a talking-to. And then I taught. I was so anxious
about my condition that I did my best to overcompensate. It
was a good class. But I didn't feel good about it.

And another late night came to mind, when after a certain hour—midnight? one A.M.?—the mood shifted. This
was often the case. Gone was the collective good cheer of
early evening, when the room was alive and packed and
thrumming. Later, something somber could creep in and take
hold. That night, late, in a nearly empty bar, I found myself
having a heart-to-heart with Cory, the Southerner, and I was
taken aback when he asked me, with something that sounded
like genuine concern, "What the hell are you doing hanging
out here?" He took a long swig of beer. "You're too young for
this shit, Rosie. It's fucking boring."

I ordered another Jameson and tried to shrug off his question. I didn't look at him. I lit another cigarette and stared at
the back of the bar, at the rows and rows of bottles that now

looked so obviously *male*, so undeniably martial. For the first time at Puffy's, I felt a little ashamed of myself, and even though Cory had meant well—was candid, anyway, had gotten *real* with me, which had come as a shock in the world of the bar, where, ideally, things stay on the surface, superficial, in a good and necessary way, no matter how much you genuinely care about the people around you—I even felt slightly rejected. Did he want me to stop coming? Or was he just warning me, with some self-deprecation and even generosity, of what might come to pass if I kept this up? At the time, he certainly didn't seem satisfied with the way things had panned out for him.

I didn't know what to say. What would I have said? That I found it totally not boring? That this bar, and the people in it, had somehow become the center of my life? It was true, but suddenly I couldn't ignore that in this there was quite possibly some authentic pathos. Why—at least up to this point, at least until I was asked directly—did this feel like home, and why did these people feel like *my* people? What did it mean that I felt happier and more accepted in this place—this bar—with these people, mostly men nearly a generation older than me, than I did with my peers, than I did, at the time, anywhere else? Why was I turning down other social opportunities—dinners with old friends, concerts, readings, etc.—to sit, night after night, on a barstool in the front corner of Puffy's Tavern? By then, I was socializing

with my Puffy's friends to the exclusion of nearly everyone
else, mostly at the bar, but also at their homes, at restaurants,
at parties, at their art openings, at their performances.

There is a particular kind of anxiety that can afflict bar
regulars, and it borders on the pathological. You go to your
bar night after night. And, night after night, the same things
happen: The same people turn up, the same conversations
are had, and, with some variations, the same stories are told.
The same booze is drunk. The same songs are played over
and over on the jukebox. One night is almost an exact replica
of the one that preceded it. Stick around long enough, show
up often enough, and you'll hear the same jokes—though
you might politely pretend that you haven't. This consistency,
this sameness, plays a big part in the comfort of regularhood.
And yet, you worry. You worry that if you fail to put in an
appearance some night, *you might miss something.* Maybe
that night—the night you decided to study instead, or to go
to a movie, or to take the time to cook a real dinner and stay
in, or maybe to hang out with people your own age—you'd
miss *something*, something funny, something moving, something important. You could be rational about it. You could
assure yourself that, really, you'd miss nothing new. But
something nags at you, something tells you that, if nothing
else, you'd just miss the placeness of the place. Think a little
deeper, and you realize that the bar has imposed a kind of
order on your life, and even if it might be a destructive one, it

is preferable to no order at all. And if you let yourself get personal about it, even a little sentimental, you tell yourself that most of all, same old same old or not, you'd miss the people, and you'd hope that they missed you, too. And you wouldn't be wrong about any of this.

What I could no longer deny after that night with Cory was that the unstudied cosmopolitan dissolution that had charmed me so in many of my fellow drinkers at Puffy's had a contagious quality, and I wasn't quite ready for it to claim me completely. I had not only fallen for this place, I'd fallen in love with the people in it. Fortunately, it was worth it; some of the people I met at that bar remain, to this day, among my closest friends. But it was time to move on. New York is a big city, after all. There were other bars. There were other people. Besides, even among my fellow regulars, a general weariness had set in, and everybody seemed to sense that this party—to which I'd arrived so late—was now officially over. There was talk of people moving out west. Of people taking full-time jobs with benefits. Of giving up cigarettes. Of drinking less.

And among those who still wanted to drink, who still needed this bar culture, this café society, a migration was underway—and it led just a few blocks north and east to some new place on West Broadway. More and more often, Jimmy would swing by Puffy's for a couple drinks in the early evening and then announce, clearly bored and a little

exasperated, "Well, that's it. I'm heading over to No-Name."
Traitor, I thought. But I understood why he was tired of it.

I was getting tired, too. I felt as though, among my very
grown-up friends at Puffy's, I, too, had grown up, and it had
happened there. I had badly wanted to be part of this world
of art openings and dinner parties, poets and painters, performance artists and playwrights, and I got what I wanted.
But I also felt that I'd not only grown up, I'd also grown old,
and before my time. In a year at Puffy's, I went from being a
chatty young drinker who could hold her own with the big
boys to a person anxiously stepping into adulthood with an
aversion to responsibility and a hell of a hangover. And the
small tragedy of being precocious is that, by definition, you
outgrow it. A single solid year at Puffy's had aged me. I could
feel it in my skin, and I could feel it in my soul. I wasn't ready
for that, but I was ready to move on. Maybe just in very small
steps, but at least as far as another bar.

7.

ED

Liquor Store Bar, New York City

Because of the rats, in the summer of 1996, I'd get home from work and trade in my sandals for a pair of tough, thick-soled hiking boots—the scarred survivors of four Vermont winters—no matter how stupid they looked with a sundress. New York summer weather is usually miserable, but in TriBeCa, where construction projects seemed to be underway on every block—converting old loft buildings into expensive condos—the dust kicked up by the jackhammers and the power of all those generators magnified the sticky, sweaty, wretched haze and made it all feel even worse. And the construction brought out the rats in force, so I'd stomp in those huge heavy boots, lest one or two brazen little bastards dared skitter across my feet, to and from my sublet apartment all the way west on Harrison Street, along the cobbled and badly lit streets of the neighborhood, past Puffy's up at the next corner, past the restaurants Chanterelle and Nobu, where limos queued up to drop off big spenders, past the Fourth Estate, the magical store on Hudson that traded in precious Persian carpets and international magazines, where the amiable owner listened to opera on the stereo and offered visitors a glass of wine, past the Greek diner and the Korean grocer, across North Moore Street, past Walker's bar and restaurant at Varick Street.

I loved those streets. How well I'd come to know them, how confidently I felt like they were mine. I wasn't afraid of the dark alleys that shot off the side streets like rusted spokes; I was young, and on good days I felt invincible. I had fallen madly back in love with the city where I was born. One more block east, past the firehouse, and then across the street and a tiny backtrack south, to the corner of West Broadway and White Street, and there, at the end of this zigzag circuit through the neighborhood, was Liquor Store—the bar for which I'd all but abandoned Puffy's, on the ground floor of an 1825 vintage, landmarked, whitewashed Federal-style townhouse with a gabled black gambrel roof.

After a year in the apartment I'd nicknamed Bleak House, I'd lucked out in finding new quarters just a block from Puffy's Tavern, the bar where I had spent the great majority of the previous three hundred and sixty-five nights of my life. But by then, I'd started to grow weary of Puffy's. I wasn't the only one. Several Puffy's regulars had already started drifting a few blocks away to Liquor Store or, as some insisted on calling it, the No-Name Bar. (In its first few months of existence it didn't have a name, and some people preferred it that way.)

Its charms could not be denied. Liquor Store was the sunny *allegro* to Puffy's dark *penseroso*. It was well worth trekking a few extra rat-filled streets to get there, straight past many other bars to which my allegiance might have shifted. But Liquor Store stood out from the corner saloons, the taverns with dartboards and pool tables, the endless variations on Irish pubs that dotted the city. It wasn't a dive, nor was it pretentious. It was just right.

Like Puffy's, Liquor Store occupied a TriBeCa corner, but unlike Puffy's, it was a southwest-facing corner, with excellent afternoon light and, in warmer weather, outdoor tables. Inside it was equally bright and simple: white walls, an oak bar with brass fittings, simple café tables and chairs, an almost total absence of clutter on the walls. The low ceilings made it feel safe and intimate. Although many of the faces were familiar, the atmosphere was strikingly different; physically, anyway, it was a far better facsimile of European café society than Puffy's. And, as at Puffy's, there was no shortage of homegrown artists, but at Liquor Store, they were joined by European expats—designers, craftsmen, performers, architects, art dealers, English, Danish, German, Irish—making for a more international crowd, on both sides of the bar, and a better mix of young and old, men and women. And there were lawyers and law students, local rogues, a tugboat captain, a burlesque revivalist, bankers, kitchen workers from the nearby restaurants, poets—a little cross section of the world below Canal Street.

I couldn't help drifting over there, too. Puffy's had given me comfort and security, but it had become routine. And I was certain the friends I'd made there, the ones I loved most, were firmly fixed in my life. I would not lose them by drinking elsewhere—especially if many of them had already decided to drink at the same elsewhere. We needed, and found, a change of scenery. If there was any dissent at Liquor Store, any factionalism, I never felt it. Here, everyone seemed so unfailingly and effortlessly pleased to see one another, so easy, so comfortable.

Well, almost everyone. On one of my earliest visits, some time before that summer, the first person I saw was *that guy*. That wiry, skinny, sour-faced, scowling, sort-of-old son-of-a-bitch with the thick black glasses and shitty teeth, a Marlboro always dangling limply from between his lips, as though it were stuck there, part of his long, lined face. An artist of some kind, apparently. Jimmy had introduced us once at Puffy's, not long before. That night, he didn't so much say anything as just kind of grunt to acknowledge my existence. And then, when he and Jimmy moved a few barstools away, I heard Jimmy whisper to him, "She's pretty, right?"

And I heard him reply, "Yeah, but too big."

Well fuck you, you toothless old motherfucker, I thought.

So when I saw him sitting there at Liquor Store early that

summer, I was less than thrilled, and my defenses went up. Cory and Jimmy and a couple of other, less familiar guys were with him at a table. Someone made an introduction.

"We've met," I said coolly. He just looked at me, unblinking, cigarette dangling, eyelids heavy, nodded, just sat there and gave me a good once-over. I felt exposed and hated being scrutinized like this. What did my friends see in this guy? He sure as hell didn't say much. And all my Puffy's friends who'd gravitated to the new place seemed to swarm around him, like he was king of the goddamned universe. I'd never seen these guys, many of whom I'd been drinking with for a solid year by then, quite like this before; they just couldn't get enough of this guy. At least three of them claimed to be his best friend. I wondered why anyone would want that. Liquor Store, whatever else it may have been—an expat refuge, a peaceable kingdom—was also Ed's second living room. And I understood that if I still wanted the company of these other men, these other drinkers, I would have to put up with him.

That summer I had started the weirdest job I ever briefly held down. I worked in the library of a paranormal research organization, based in a grand brick-and-limestone townhouse on the Upper West Side. It paid next to nothing, but I didn't have to do much. A few days a week, I sat behind a massive desk in a wood-paneled, dusty, magnificently moody library that readily imparted the not unpleasant illusion of being trapped inside a Gothic novel, filed a bit, shelved and reshelved books, and fielded questions from the public—the credulous and incredulous both. One visitor, who'd been eighty-sixed by the organization previously for erratic behavior, sometimes showed up in shambolic disguises—floppy hat, pasted-on beard, trench coat, that sort of thing—to regain access to arcane texts on ESP or something. Far more poignant was the young widow, earnest in her desperate longing to make contact, somehow, with her departed husband, as though there must be some book in our collection that would show the way. Skeptics called and tried to squeeze confessions out of me: Did I really believe in this? Really? Well, I didn't know, and it didn't matter to me. It was a job, and a pretty cushy one at that, and mostly I read.

The library's holdings were all over the place. There was plenty on hauntings and automatic writing and mediums and how to bend spoons with your mental energy, but there were also books about the Shakers, about American spiritualist movements, and mythology and folklore. I particularly relished the works of one Vance Randolph, who collected Ozark songs and stories, a good many of which were bawdy, scatological, or just flat-out raunchy, with titles like "A Good Dose of Clap" and "The Prick Teaser."

So after a day among the dead and the undead and the mystics and the psychics, I'd look forward to a few Jamesons down at Liquor Store. Most of my drinking mates knew about my job and would tease me, in a good-natured way, about it. I got used to questions like, "Hey Rosie, bust any ghosts today?" "Bend any silverware . . . *with your mind*?"

And in turn I might tell them about the visiting Girl Scouts—
one of whom, a pallid, dark-haired preadolescent with a disconcertingly serious countenance, seemed to have *it*, the
ability to move objects with sheer psychic will. Or I'd tell
them about the ectoplasm "samples" I'd seen pictures of,
specimens that looked like nothing so much as gnarly swaths
of snotted-up cheesecloth.

Ed seemed vaguely interested in all this. But he only
really started paying attention when I mentioned that I'd
been reading dirty stories from the Ozarks.

"Oh yeah?" he said, like he knew something about them.
"From the Ozarks?"

"Yeah," I answered, still a little defensive around him.
"They were collected by this folklorist Vance Randolph—"

"Shit!" He smiled big, baring those insane teeth unself-
consciously, which seldom happened. *"You know who that
guy is?"*

Well, I felt like I'd won a prize, and in a way, I had. It's
not that I really had wanted to crack this guy, to break
through somehow—I saw no reason to make a special
effort—but now that I had, I knew that I could feel more
relaxed in his unavoidable company, and that my status as a
Liquor Store regular was on more solid ground. Ed was from
Missouri, it turned out, though he kept his past, his provenance, his history, more than a little mysterious. (I later
learned from Jimmy that he claimed to have been conceived
on a Greyhound bus, and also to have once been abducted by

Gypsies.) And now it was as though Ed and I were meeting again for the first time. We'd struck on an unlikely contact point. His earlier insult, if not quite forgotten, had receded, and suddenly we were off—on a long, rambling conversation that went on until late. He had a deep voice, and after nearly thirty years in New York, he had not lost a distinct Missouri twang. But I did most of the talking.

What became clear to me that night was that what distinguished Ed from so many of the men I drank with was this: He was a listener. A great, patient, attentive listener. It didn't matter if I was telling him a convoluted story that trailed off into nowhere, or something more painful and personal that I would share with few other people. He listened. As much as I valued the light and fluid back-and-forth of bar conversation, the ensemble rhythms of Dublin *craíc*, the free exchange of bad jokes and friendly teasing and testy argument that were so much a part of my previous bar experiences and so much a part of what I love about bars, in the act of pure listening Ed gave me something different and deeper and, at the time, more necessary. What had seemed like arrogance to me at first was something altogether different: an active interest in what others were saying and doing, and a talent for taking it all in. By the end of the night, I not only felt more certain that I belonged at this bar, but that I'd gotten to know someone of unusual depth and intelligence.

And so it was for most of the summer of 1996, night after night, having put in my time at the library, I'd swing by the sublet, change the footwear, run the rat gauntlet, and head to Liquor Store. On the best nights, when there was no rain and the heat had abated and maybe there was just a little breeze, the regulars would collect at the tables outside and look down West Broadway to the luminous view of the World Trade Center. Most of my life I'd thought those buildings were so ugly, but from there, from that seat outside the bar, they were so impressive, all lit up as the sun set. And we'd watch the rats dart around the corner and into the grates under the sidewalk, like it was a spectator sport. I'd always run into at least some of my Puffy's friends there, plus the expats—supercool Adam, an English painter in skinny black jeans and skinny black T-shirts with a jolt of white hair that vee'd into a sharp widow's peak on his forehead (earning him the nickname the Prince of Darkness), the laddish British furniture restorers drinking pint after pint, the comically laconic Danish businessman always a little scruffy in his wrinkled suits, maybe even the tugboat captain with a penchant for fancy restaurants.

I loved both of the Irish bartenders, one a little gruff but also warm and funny; the other no-nonsense at first, but engaging and interested once you got to know him, and protective of his regulars. I enjoyed all of them, but as I approached the bar and scanned the sidewalk tables, or peeked through the window, there was really only one person I wanted to see. I'd walk over hoping Ed would be there, practically praying that he would be. And if he was, I was relieved and happy and all felt okay with the world. If he wasn't, well, I might just turn around and go back to Puffy's instead.

I was so uncertain then of the shape my life might take, and often fretful. I was still in graduate school, but paying it less and less mind all the time. And of course the bar was where I went to forget all that, to stop fretting, to drink and talk and put on my cheeriest possible front. At the bar, you don't so much unload your shit as set it aside. You keep the conversation light; wit is welcome, humor even more valued, but nothing too deep, nothing too serious. Of course, there is the tradition of the stranger who shows up and spills his guts. And then, having confessed all, absolved by the proxy priest-hood of the barman, the stranger moves on. I have on one occasion been that stranger, at a bar I'd never visited before and never returned to after. But as a regular, that's really not what one does. There's safety in superficiality, in not letting things get too deep or too personal. The bar, usually, is a blessed refuge from the too-deep and too-personal. But my instincts told me that with Ed, I could, and should, get personal. I could talk, I could vent—about work and family and worry—and he would listen, and take it seriously, without issuing judgment or prescription. I knew that as soon as I saw him, as soon as we hugged—and he hugged with great strength and heartbreaking delicacy all at once—I would feel fine. And then I could spend the next hour or two talking his ear off; he would nod, he would focus, he would be absolutely, completely there.

So of course by then, I got why all these guys had such deep affection for him. Ed clearly didn't like everybody. But if he liked you, well, he *really* liked you. And if he didn't, well, good luck to you. I can't say exactly that he held many people in contempt. I don't think that's what it was, but often, he sure looked like he did. If he took to you, he made it clear. It wasn't hard to tell that he was happy to see you. In the way he called out your name. Or extended a barstool or chair to you. Or threw his arms around you and embraced you with his usual disarming tenderness.

After our inauspicious start, we had become fast friends. And after finding him so unappealing at first, I now found him singularly beautiful. I wasn't sure that it was romantic love, exactly; I wasn't sure *what* it was. I think many of us— Ed's drinking friends—were a little bit in some kind of love with him. But I suspect that because I was a woman in this company of men, I felt I had to think harder about this. I didn't especially want to have a crush on a drinking buddy. Particularly a married drinking buddy. I told myself it was fine; my crush on Ed was probably no different from the man-crushes so many of the guys seemed to have on him.

But one night something happened. It was a charmed night: Everyone was happy, the little room thick with smoke and full of laughter. I was sitting at a table with Ed and Jimmy and a couple of other guys. Ed and I got into some kind of loud argument. I have no memory of what we were fighting about, but suddenly we were standing up, palms planted on the little table, screaming at each other. And then, just as suddenly, we kissed, right across the table. It was quick. Just as quickly, we backed away from each other. It was nothing, and it was something. The room's din died down, everything went into a spin for a moment, then stopped. I knew that it would never happen again, and it shouldn't. Jimmy sat there gaping. I was pretty sure he'd give me shit about it some day, even if he never said a thing about it to Ed.

I didn't return to the bar the next night. It wasn't that I was avoiding Ed—I never wanted to avoid him—but I was afraid that maybe he would now think less of me. Two nights later I was ready to return. I had to. Liquor Store was where I lived in the off-hours and, besides, regardless of what had happened—a small thing that had now become overblown, amplified, outsized in my conscience—I still had to see Ed.

I ran into him before I even got to the bar. He was walking across North Moore Street, too, and when I saw him from half a block away, I picked up my pace and caught up with him. "Hey Ed." I nodded.

"Rosie." He nodded.

We said nothing more. We proceeded to Liquor Store, where he ordered a beer and I ordered a Jameson. And it felt like everything was completely back to normal—like it had never *not* been normal. There would never be another kiss, and that was a good thing. Instead, there would be more talking, more listening, more drinking, and a greater deepening of our friendship. If anything, things were easier now, like some air had been let out.

Summer was nearly shifting into fall, and my time in the sublet was running out. I couch-surfed in the neighborhood for a while. I started looking at apartments in Manhattan, but there was nothing I could afford. A friend told me that there was an apartment available in the building next door to her in Brooklyn. I didn't want to move to Brooklyn. Really, I didn't want to leave a ten-block radius of Liquor Store. But I went and checked the place out. It was a real apartment, with space and light and closets and high ceilings, and the price was right, and friends lived next door. In October I moved in, knowing that I wouldn't be able to spend as much time at Liquor Store, knowing that I wouldn't be able to see Ed nearly as often. But I felt that now, with a place of my own and some distance from TriBeCa and its bars, my life would start to stabilize. And it did. For a while I was happy to set up house and refinish the floors and paint the walls and scavenge for furniture and cook real dinners. I missed the almost-nightly sessions at Liquor Store, but I felt ready to start acting like an adult, or something. And maybe adulthood was finally ready for me.

That fall, in dizzyingly rapid succession, I got an apartment, I got a cat, and I got involved with a really good, really smart guy. Someone my own age. Someone I didn't know from a bar. Frank and I had met during graduate school orientation the previous year and slowly became friends. We wound up in a few classes together—Spenser; Yeats and Linguistics; Revolutionary Poetics. We taught at the same community college, where we, as brand-new professors, were in the same small group of teachers who had to meet weekly with a supervisor who helped us figure out how to do our job. In these meetings and in our classes together, Frank impressed me. Whenever he spoke in our seminars, he did so judiciously: the points he made were always insightful and nuanced, never gratuitous, never uttered just to show off. He was an excellent reader with a broad and interesting mind, and a fine writer. And in our little teaching group, I also discovered that he was a stand-up guy with a strong sense of justice. Once, when one of the other male students in the group launched a vicious verbal attack on one of the women in the group—disagreements about pedagogy could get heated, but I'd never heard anything like this—Frank cleared his throat and calmly said, "I doubt you'd talk this way to me. Or to any other man." The perpetrator was silenced. No one in the room would ever forget that. We all knew that Frank was right. Much as I wished I'd said it, I was glad he had. My respect for him multiplied, and I'm pretty sure that's exactly when I started to fall in love. Not long after that, we tried to make a plan to see a movie together, but couldn't figure it out. In December, he mentioned that he was having a small birthday dinner at one of my favorite restaurants in Chinatown. I promptly invited myself. And that's when and where our romance really began—over platters of duck with flowering chives, Singapore mai fun, clams with black beans, and roast pork with ginger-scallion sauce.

Normal things were happening in my life, which surprised me, and I think it also surprised many of my bar friends. Not long after Frank and I had started dating, I took him to meet my Puffy's and Liquor Store friends, and I soon felt pretty terrible about subjecting him to their scrutiny. But it was necessary, because these people had become like another family to me. Frank was low-key and often shy, a generally mild-mannered, even-tempered academic. Some members of my bar family were friendly and open and welcoming. Some just tried to take a reading of him, like they were checking out a horse at auction. And others, just a few, were downright hostile. One especially tart-tongued friend grabbed him by the shoulders and looked him right in the eyes: "If you fuck with this girl," she said, "I will superglue your hand to your dick." I tried to laugh it off, but I could tell that he hadn't found it funny.

Part of me was moved by how protective some of my friends were. And part of me felt uncomfortable, even resentful, and it made me wonder if maybe some among them didn't want me to get on with my life, to behave like a normal person in her twenties probably should, as if I should just stay put in this little world of bars, drinking every night, occasionally fucking men whom I did not love, with whom it was understood there would be no future. I knew something serious was happening in my life, and I knew that such seriousness fits uneasily into bar culture. Ultimately I didn't really care what most of the crowd thought of my boyfriend, as long as they were courteous and not too scary. But I *did* care what Ed thought. I trusted him. I trusted his judgment. I knew he didn't like everybody. His approval mattered.

So when Frank and I went to Liquor Store together one evening, I did a quick check through the window to see if Ed was there. He was. I took a deep breath and collected myself, like we were about to have an audience with the Godfather, and we walked inside. I'd told Frank about Ed. I'd gushed about him. He knew that it was important to me that they meet.

I introduced them. They shook hands. We sat down. Not much was said. A few questions. A few answers. They were both quiet men. I felt tense and a little awkward. I made some small talk, mostly about how great they both were, as though it were a public relations event or a diplomatic summit. I talked up Ed's art and Frank's scholarship, both of which I ardently admired. But the point was to get them talking to each other, and that wasn't happening. What would get them going? There had to be something. Finally, it hit me: It had been Missouri folklore that had brought Ed and me together, the night we became friends. The Show-Me State would come to the rescue once again.

"Frank, Ed's a big Twain fan," I said casually. Frank was,

too, even though Mark Twain was well out of the realm of his academic specialization in English Romanticism. But that was all it took. For fun, Frank had recently reread *Pudd'nhead Wilson* for the first time in years, and he and Ed had found their subject. Now I could sit back for a spell and just listen. Perfect.

Frank and I had a couple of drinks and left. Everything seemed to have gone fine, but I wasn't sure what Ed thought.

"He's cool, right?" I asked Frank.

"Yeah," Frank agreed. "He's cool. And really smart."

Not long after their first meeting, Frank arrived at Liquor Store before me one night. He later told me that Ed had grilled him. "He wanted to make sure my intentions were honorable," Frank told me. He said that they were. Frank was touched by Ed's concern, and relieved that no threats to his person had been made.

The next time I returned to Liquor Store by myself I found Ed alone at a table. I got a whiskey and joined him. He nodded and said quietly, "He's a nice young man." I already knew that, but I needed to hear it from Ed.

I'd still stop by the bar now and then after work, but my visits became rarer. I was starting a new life, one that relied less on the bar. But on a bright sunny spring day in 1998, Frank and I found ourselves in TriBeCa and headed to Liquor Store. We ran into Ed a block south of the bar, on West Broadway. He was unusually worked up, uncharacteristically loquacious. He delivered a rapid-fire monologue. He and his wife had been in New Mexico. "It was weird, man. Even went to Roswell. Looked at some property. Checked some shit out." He'd finally gotten around to seeing a dentist. And he'd been to the doctor, for the first time in years. Something was wrong. There would be some kind of operation. But he'd be okay, he assured us. I told him that Frank and I were planning our first trip together, to Europe. His parents were living in Bayreuth for a year. "Well, if you're going to Munich, let me know," Ed said. "I have people there."

Later, I called Ed. Sure, we'd go to Munich, an easy train ride from Bayreuth. We'd need to get away from the parents for a few days. We talked for nearly an hour. "Go to my gallery, on Maximilianstrasse. And go to my friend's restaurant, near the market. And drink at Schumann's. Use my name," he said. "And yeah, the museums. You should go to those, too." I jotted all the names and numbers down in a notebook. Thanks to Ed, Frank and I spent three wonderful days in Munich, meeting Ed's friends, eating and drinking in places where he was as beloved as he was at Liquor Store. But the best and most revealing part of our visit to Munich was seeing his art there. At his gallery, an assistant patiently pulled drawings from the flat files and reverently showed us fine, funny drawings, funny and tough and tender, mostly in black with occasional shots of other colors, spare but not at all stingy—beautiful in an off-center way, a way that makes you stop and think about what beauty is, anyway, not unlike their maker. *This is where Ed really abides,* I remember thinking,

in his work. This is who he is. This is where all of that listening,
all of that reception, all of that quietness and patience, all of that
toughness and discernment go.

But by that November, something else was wrong. I'd
heard through the grapevine that Ed had been diagnosed
with cancer. Really bad, advanced cancer that had started in
one organ and metastasized elsewhere. Soon after I heard the
news, I caught up with him at Liquor Store. He wasn't smoking anymore. I wasn't sure what to say to him, and neither, it
seemed, were most of the guys. They were clearly distraught,
but trying to act like everything was okay, or was going to be
okay. It was unusually quiet around the bar. After that, he
was in and out of the hospital.

I called him at the hospital a few times, and his voice
was weaker with every conversation. "Don't visit," he said
emphatically. He'd told others the same thing. He didn't
want visitors; he didn't want people to see him like that—
other than his wife and the doctors. I talked to people about
it. I couldn't stand thinking that I might never see him again.
I wanted to respect his wishes. But I was also scared. What
would I say? I couldn't imagine treading lightly around Ed. I
knew that would piss him off. And in the face of death, I was
suddenly, weirdly, shamefully timid. I stayed away. And when
he died, less than five months after he'd been diagnosed, I
regretted it. But even Jimmy—the best of all those who made
the claim of being Ed's best friend—had obeyed his wishes.

There was a round of phone calls one day in late March

1999. Ed had died. And as much as I expected a call, as much as I knew it was coming, the news punched me in the gut. I hated that I hadn't gone to see him. I hated even more that he was gone. Ed had only been part of my life for a short time. Should that have made his loss harder or easier to bear? I couldn't tell. I knew how crushed Jimmy, who'd known Ed for thirty years, since they were boys—"we're still boys," Jimmy once said—must have been. They had traveled the world together, working for a famous artist. They had spent mornings drawing together on a hotel balcony in Hawaii. They had been poor, grubby young artists together in Manhattan in the seventies. During the course of their friendship, they had seen each other through odd jobs and successes and failures, through girlfriends, through their courtships and marriages, through everything. I tried to imagine how he must have felt, the enormity of the loss. At the same time, I was jealous. He'd had decades of Ed; I'd only had a few years.

In my cubicle at work the next day, I cried. I'd recently left graduate school and was pretty new to my job at a publishing company. My coworkers busily passed by. I wanted to shake them, explain to them that, really, I wasn't hysterical, but something *hugely important* had happened. But there was copy to edit, there were faxes to send, there were phone calls to make, there was shit to do. I went to the office of one colleague whom I'd become friendly with and told her that a friend had died.

"He was the most amazing person I've ever known," I told her. "And a great artist. A *really* great artist."

She said she was sorry about my loss. "How did you know him?"

"From the bar," I said.

She was not unsympathetic, but she looked a little puzzled. Like it was strange that I should be so invested in someone I knew from a bar, someone I drank with. I hadn't grown up with Ed. He was not a relative, though he was family in a way that was suddenly too hard to explain. We had not gone to school together. We had never worked together. We knew each other because, night after night, for just a couple of years, we drank in each other's company. Something felt uncomfortably snobbish about my coworker's puzzlement, as though the affinities upon which friendships are based should be prescribed by having gone to the same school or working in the same field, as though having a friend who was male and significantly older was somehow suspect, as though having a bar in common was not an acceptable foundation for true friendship.

And part of me understood my coworker's puzzlement, because I knew that what I'd wanted—at least what I *thought* I'd wanted—from bar life was something both real and less than real, a kind of controlled, convivial shallowness. The bar was not where one went to get deep, nor certainly to cultivate the kinds of friendships that might someday lead to hard, horrible mourning. It is convenient to compartmentalize, and I have frequently done just that: There are friends, and there are *bar* friends. Clearly, in Ed's case, the line had blurred. And I couldn't imagine missing anyone more.

Jimmy got busy organizing the first of two memorial services. This one would be casual, at a larger bar right across the street from Liquor Store. He called me a few nights before the memorial and asked if I wanted to read something. Yes, of course I did. But it took me a while to figure out what. I thought back to the first time Ed and I really talked—the long night of whiskey and cigarettes and Ozark folklore. I recalled how when we met, I was working in the paranormal library, how I'd told him about the young widow who repeatedly visited, wanting so earnestly to communicate with her departed beloved. And I remembered reading, somewhere, a letter Twain had written, in which he spoke of friendship:

> I remember you & recall you *without effort, without exercise of will*;—that is, by *natural impulse*, undictated by a sense of duty, or of obligation. And that, I take it, is the only sort of remembering worth the having. When we think of friends, & call their faces out of the shadows & their voices out of the echoes that faint along the corridors of memory, & do it without knowing *why*, save that we *love* to do it, we may content ourselves that that friendship is a Reality, & not a Fancy—that it is builded upon a rock, & not

upon the sands that dissolve away with the ebbing tides &
carry their monuments with them.

About a dozen people spoke at the memorial. Jimmy went
first. He ended his talk by describing Ed's hugs. "Did you
ever hug Ed?" he asked. "It was like one of his sculptures"—
here, his deep voice cracked—"fragile, but still strong, and
still very beautiful." Exactly. I read the Twain. And it's true:
It takes no effort to think on Ed. It is all natural impulse, and
I do love to do it, even as it still breaks my heart.

At home that night, hours after the memorial, Frank and
I were in bed, and I started to cry again. "You know," I said,
as though it were a confession, "I was madly in love with him."

"I know," Frank said, with no anger, no jealousy, no surprise, only understanding. "I know." I wondered if it had
been that obvious to everyone.

I thought back to that summer when I first got to know
Ed, when I first noticed that here was someone rare, someone I could rely on, someone who was more to me than just a
drinking companion. I thought of the widow at the paranormal library, how I'd been moved by, but also dismissive
of, her hopeless yearning to make contact with her dead husband. Now that I had lost someone I loved—someone who
was not a relative, someone I'd chosen to be part of my life—
I understood her better, and felt ashamed that I'd ever been
dismissive of her quest.

After Ed died, I sometimes went back to Liquor Store. If I had to pick a favorite New York bar, it was the one. It hit the sweet spot: I was in it, I was of it, I was happy to be there, but I never felt I'd gotten in too deep, never felt obligated to put in an appearance. I don't recall ever getting crazy drunk there, ever losing it, ever being appallingly fucked up—well, *once* maybe—ever leaving wishing I hadn't gone that night. I always was there because I *wanted* to be there. There was no pressure. I did stop by a few days before my wedding in 2002. The usual suspects, mostly married guys in their forties and fifties, were there at the bar. I announced that my wedding was the following weekend and asked for the best marriage advice they could offer. "Go ahead," I said. "Lay it on me."

"Separate bars, darling," a furniture restorer, one of the British lads, shouted back. "Separate bars."

When Liquor Store closed in 2005 after a drawn-out battle with neighbors who objected to its outdoor seating, part of me mourned its passing, but part of me was fine with it, because I felt that without Ed, the place just hadn't really been itself anyway. Despite the presence of many familiar drinking associates, it was too empty, and too painful.

And all these years later, I still think about Ed all the time—every day, really—and no matter how many excellent drinking companions I'd come to know since then, I've never found another person whose company I'd rather have at the bar. Jimmy and I don't hang out together nearly as much as we used to, but we do run into each other once in a while.

And *whenever* we do, every single time, like we can't stop ourselves, because we really can't, we talk about Ed. My failure to visit Ed in the hospital still haunts me. Jimmy insists that I did right by obeying his wishes. I'll never be sure. But when we get past that discussion, we get back to what exactly it was about the guy that made us love him so intensely. We've tried to figure out why it is that we still talk about him constantly, what made him a drinking companion unlike any other. "He just made me feel special," Jimmy told me not long ago while we shared a bottle of wine. "Maybe because there were so many people he *didn't* want to talk to."

We clinked our glasses.

Here's to you, then, you toothless old motherfucker, I thought. *How I wish you hadn't up and died on us.*

"He made me feel special, too," I said. "I felt really lucky to be loved by Ed."

"You *were* lucky," Jimmy said.

I was.

8.

BAR CHAPLAIN

The Fish Bar, New York City

My friend Paul—barman, scholar, and gentleman, previously of Puffy's Tavern and sundry other drinking establishments—pulled me aside at the holiday party Frank and I threw in 1999. His cheeks were flushed and his spirit elevated after a few cups of glögg—that irresistible Scandinavian winter delight composed of red wine, vodka, and brandy, slowly, slowly, slowly brought to a simmer with orange peels, cloves, and cardamom.

"You know what I want?" he asked me, quietly but excitedly, almost in a whisper. *More glögg,* I might have guessed. But that wasn't it. "I want to have a bar," he said, "where a woman could come in, sit down with a book, read, have a drink, and not be bothered." He was excited to open, finally, after so many years of pulling pints and mixing martinis at other people's bars, a place of his own (or almost his own; he had a partner in his friend and fellow bartender John, an acerbic Welshman and former rock-and-roll roadie).

The following month the two took over the space for-
merly occupied by an old dive on Fifth Street in the East Village, rechristened it the Fish Bar, and opened for business.
The place was tiny, with a bar that seated about eight, a banquette for about ten more against the back wall, and a few
wobbly two-top tables in between. It was dark and cramped,
and efforts had been made to liven it up with a nautical
theme. Sometimes the seafarer scheme—in bluish greens
and greenish blues, with anchors, and arty fish, and coral and
shells, etc. etc. etc.—gave me the unsettling sensation that I
was getting drunk in a boy's nursery. But I could get past
that. We were there because of Paul, and because of the environment he created.

Yes, here was a place where a lone woman might stop by,
sit herself down at the bar, and quietly read, reasonably confident that no drunks would menace her (though one might
buy her a drink), where the prices were right, where the bartenders knew what they were doing. Frank and I felt at home
there right away, alongside a handful of holdovers from the
previous bar and other drinkers who, like us, had followed
Paul and John to their new place, and a few strangers who
wouldn't stay strangers for long—the cute young couple consisting of a chef and a painter, a lanky and affable middle-
aged interior designer with a litany of health problems, and
an argumentative cartographer.

Conveniently, I was still working at the publishing company, only a few blocks west of the bar, though I was starting

to have other ideas about what I might do with my life. The Fish Bar was a perfect after-work spot, where, more often than not, Frank would meet up with me after his day's work—writing his dissertation—had wound down, too. We might break up our evenings with a bite somewhere in the neighborhood, return to the Fish Bar for a nightcap (or two), and then make our way back to Brooklyn. We had settled into a comfortable domestic groove, and Paul and John's little place felt like an extension of our home.

Whenever we had friends visiting from out of town, we'd take them there, and they were consistently struck—moved, even—by the uncommon sweetness of the place, the family feeling, the friendliness and warmth. The size and scale of the bar made it difficult not to be sociable there, elbow to elbow. This was a place where people could grow old together, as domesticated as an East Village bar could be. On Sunday afternoons, Paul's girlfriend brought in cheese and sausage for all to share, and one of the bartenders frequently showed up with pies he'd baked from scratch. There were regular cookoffs—chili, pasta—to which regulars and staff alike would bring in their best dishes. There were spirited trivia nights, which Frank and I were politely asked to sit out of after we'd brought in a ringer—my know-it-all cousin Phil—a few times too many. We honored the request.

I was getting restless at work. The hours were long, the pay was low, I had no ambitions of advancing in the company, and this nagging feeling that I needed to do something more *meaningful* was starting to get to me. I'd been taking adult education Hebrew classes at the Jewish seminary across the street from my office and volunteering at the soup kitchen they operated on Monday nights. By the time I got to the cafeteria, meal service was over, and all that remained for me to do was the cleaning up. I was sorry I didn't get to cook, didn't get to feed the guests, didn't get to interact with them and with the other volunteers, most of whom were also gone, or on the way out, when I arrived. But cleanup duty was fine by me. It was useful, it was purposeful. I scrubbed and scoured huge industrial-size pots until they shone, wiped down the crumb-covered tables, swept and mopped the kitchen. One evening, I ran into the young rabbinical student who taught my Hebrew class just as I was leaving. He was pleased that I'd been volunteering at the soup kitchen. "I saw the poster one evening after class," I told him, "and since it's right across the street from work, it's convenient."

"Is service supposed to be *convenient*?" he retorted with a sly smile. He wasn't being antagonistic. He was funny and, especially for a young man, wise. He'd make a great rabbi, I was sure. And he was right. He'd gotten his point across; there's nothing inherently *wrong* with volunteering when and where it's convenient to do so—it's better than not volunteering at all—but it shouldn't be anyone's major criterion for trying to do a little bit of good in the world. I couldn't get his question out of my head, and it troubled me throughout the next few days at work. I probably needed to inconvenience myself a lot more. And it's not coincidental that studying Hebrew and volunteering in the soup kitchen happened at the same location. Faith and service—both of which had always been important to me, even if the ways in which I had expressed each had taken many forms, and to which my commitment had fluctuated a lot over the years—were, in my mind and in my heart, of a piece. And both were occupying more and more of my thoughts and my time.

I started taking Hebrew not only because I believe that faith is built into the alphabet, the characters, the words, the syntax, the language itself, but also to fill a gap. I hadn't had a Bat Mitzvah, but much like I wish I'd been forced to learn piano or violin *before* my self-consciousness of my lack of musical talent had set in, much like I wish I'd learned how to drive *before* I'd become an adult and had spent too many years thinking about how fucking dangerous cars are, I wish I'd been sent to Hebrew school. (And of course I realize this is all easy for *me* to say, not having been made to turn down party invitations to practice my violin, not having been awakened early on Saturday mornings to haul my ass to temple. I know. I know.) Still, I'm grateful that I grew up in a secular home and was given the freedom—more, surely, because of my mother's lack of interest in such concerns than as a matter of some benevolent and liberal family policy—to explore religion in whatever ways I chose.

I tried to make sense of my religiosity for years, but the thing is, it's really not so complicated. It's just how I'm wired.

When I was seven or eight and spent summers with my family on Fire Island, I often went to services there by myself, walking barefoot (as most did on the island) to the little reform temple nearby, where I loved the hippie homeyness of it all, the strumming of guitars and singing of folk songs along with the reading of scriptures and reciting of prayers, and where I believed that the little cups of grape juice they served to us kids were wine until somebody set me straight. (I was also wired for wino-hood; family legend maintains that one of my first words was *Bordeaux*.) I was pretty sure I was getting kind of drunk on *something*. But even as a kid I doubted that I'd ever be a good and observant Jew; I was too curious about any and *every* religion I heard about or read about or saw something on TV about, and that was fine by my folks, if a little startling. Did I want to go to Easter mass with a Catholic friend and her family? Sure, go ahead. Quaker meeting? Why not? Buddhist sitting meditation? Fine.

It is possible, however, that the long pagan period that began in high school, peaked when I was living in the Santa Cruz mountains, and ended in college had been too trying for my mother. She was not exactly dazzled to see my byline in publications with titles like *Weekly Wiccan World*, nor especially enchanted by the chanting she could hear just behind my bedroom door. The many hours during which I commandeered the kitchen to mix up astringent tinctures and gooey poultices with strong-smelling herbs that I procured either at the dusty witchcraft book and supply shops

I frequented or by mail from farms and communes across the country caused her to raise her well-groomed eyebrows on not a few occasions. The tarot cards. The runes. The far-flung pen pals whose letters arrived in envelopes emblazoned with ankhs and pentagrams and return addresses bearing names that sounded like *Lord of the Rings* characters. The tattered, dog-eared, suspect-looking treatises about ancient mystery cults and Druidic wisdom and the healing proper-ties of plants and crystals. The little altar I set up on my bed-room dresser complete with a miniature cauldron and a chalice and a bunch of stones and dried leaves. The solemn invocations of the Old Gods. It was all a bit much for her, and, in time, it no longer satisfied my own spiritual yearn-ings, if only I could figure out exactly what they were, exactly what it was I wanted from God, or the gods, and what He or She or They in turn expected of me.

In my senior year of college, under the heady influence of William Blake, I started to think that maybe I might be a Christian—but a peculiar and specific kind of Christian, the sort of Christian I imagined Blake himself might have been. I read about and admired many of the old dissenting, rabble-rousing British sects, like the True Levellers, the Muggleton-ians, the early Methodists, the Shakers. I could get behind their radical and liberating conception of Jesus and, in many cases, their proto-communist practices and the fiery indig-nation that connected them in one long angry righteous line to the prophets of the Hebrew Bible. Similarly, I was drawn to more recent Christian thinkers who championed social and economic justice, like Martin Luther King, Jr., and Dietrich Bonhoeffer and Dorothy Day.

When I moved back to New York after college, I went to services at many of the grand old do-gooder churches—the Riverside and Saint John the Divine and the Abyssinian Baptist—and some less grand but equally impassioned houses of worship (a Methodist church in my Brooklyn neighborhood, an authentically radical Presbyterian congregation on, of all the unlikely places, the Upper East Side). I was frequently moved by the worship services I took in, roused by the hymns and spirituals, touched by the sense of community, inspired by the faith-in-action that was so palpable in these places, by the collective commitment to social justice. But I fell silent when prayers were directed specifically to Jesus, and I could not take communion. I was not, after all, a Christian. Or was I?

I agonized over this question and prayed for an answer to come. When it didn't, I started to attend Unitarian Universalist services regularly—for Unitarians make no doctrinal demands, and irrespective of the tradition's Christian roots, one can now identify as a Jewish Unitarian, a Buddhist Unitarian, even an atheist Unitarian, as one sees fit. Its tent is wide open. The sermons were always smart and learned, the congregants welcoming to newcomers and visitors like me. But it all felt so fucking *polite*. Everyone was so educated and rational. The ecstatic experience I sought could not be found there. I think I wanted a Unitarian congregation that behaved like a Pentecostal congregation. Such a thing does not exist. I envied the submissive faith I observed in the Chasidim I saw davening every morning on the subway, that I witnessed among Pentecostals. But my own skepticism was stronger than I'd reckoned. I had too many questions to allow myself to be overtaken completely by the spirit.

Yet the more I immersed myself in the spiritual life of the city, the more, inevitably, it became essential to me. By the time I'd become a regular at the Fish Bar, I was reading the Bible regularly, along with books about faith leaders I found especially compelling and inspired, figures like Digger leader Gerrard Winstanley and Shaker leader Ann Lee. And it frustrated me that here, in New York City, where all things seem possible, this place that so many people move to from *everywhere* that they might be free to express themselves creatively, sexually, socially, howsoever they wish, it remained an anomaly to make one's own way in faith. Among my largely liberal circle of friends, the fact that I even believe in God was, and is, regarded as a bit of a novelty—interrogated with courteous curiosity by some, with condescension by others, with outright contempt by a few. That I was, furthermore, a believer who could not identify exactly as a Jew or as a Christian or as a Zen Buddhist or as a Sufi, as *something*, was even harder for people to grasp.

So when in 2000 I was called—seriously called, like, by *God*—well, that threw most everybody, not least of all myself. I wish I could report that some magnificent spiritual drama attended this call, but a host of angels did not fly to my side with trumpets, nor was I struck asunder by a brilliant, near-blinding light, and no white salamander was telling me what had to be done. It was something quieter, something internal. My desire to do some good in the world, to be a servant, kept growing stronger, and I knew that this yearning was connected to my faith and believed that somehow this added up to a call to ministry. Besides, if I could not find the kind of worship I wanted—something both socially progressive and spiritually ecstatic—I would have to make it up. Maybe I could even bring a modified Muggletonian-style drinking and dissenting ministry right to the Fish Bar. The Shakers aside, teetotaling sects baffled me. If wine flowed freely in the Hebrew Bible and was good enough for Jesus, surely it was good enough for us. And if Saint Brigid had the power to turn water into whiskey, she must have had good reasons and honorable intentions.

I learned that such a thing as interfaith ministry existed, that it did not object in the least to self-described Marxist Muggletonian Jews who spent much of their time in bars. I enrolled in a part-time two-year ordination program, quit my publishing job, and went to work as a community organizer for an antipoverty nonprofit organization, where I was charged with engaging faith leaders and their congregations all over the city to work harder and advocate more to address

the needs and concerns of low-income New Yorkers. This
work brought me to fiery worship services at storefront Pentecostal churches in Brownsville where hands were laid upon
my head; to progressive Jewish congregations in Park Slope;
to fancy high-church Episcopalians on the Upper East Side
who fought for the homeless men who set up camp on their
steps, to the endless and mean-spirited consternation of their
neighbors; to meetings at which socially conservative Evan-
gelists from Staten Island, openly gay rabbis, and Jesuit priests
sat at the same table, cooperating in common cause, in service
of the greater good, in service of God, in service of the poor-
est New Yorkers. It didn't always go smoothly, but we did
manage to get some things done. And after these services and
meetings and field visits, I had the Fish Bar. Among the bar
staff, there were atheists and agnostics and Catholics, but if
anybody there found my growing dedication to God and to
service strange or foolish, they certainly didn't let on. If anything, I was sure I had their support.

On the morning of September 11, 2001, instead of heading
straight to my office in the financial district, I went to a
diner in my neighborhood to have a meeting with a local
rabbi who was active in social justice circles. It was, as anyone
who was in New York City that day will tell you, a gorgeous late summer blue-sky morning. I figured the rabbi and

I would talk for an hour or so, then I'd amble over to the local middle school to vote in the local elections that were scheduled that day, then hop on the subway and get my ass to the office. Like any ordinary day, but sunnier, and maybe more promising.

The rabbi and I ordered breakfast and I showed her a pamphlet I'd drafted that congregations could use to advocate for easier food stamp applications. We'd only really just started talking when someone in the restaurant turned the radio up louder. A waitress came by to top off our coffee, and we asked her if she wouldn't mind maybe turning it down a little, since we were trying to have a meeting. She looked dazed. "Something's going on at the World Trade Center," she told us. "Like, a plane crash." It was not yet nine A.M.

We figured that this must have been caused by an inexperienced pilot accidentally flying his plane too low, straying off course, panicking, hitting the north tower. But as everyone in the diner fell silent and listened to the grave voices on the radio, the truth of what was going on sank in, and it was more horrifying than any of us could have imagined. I was grateful at least to be in the rabbi's company. Her presence was calming and comforting. Of course she'd have to get back to her office immediately. It was possible that some of her congregants, their friends, their loved ones, were in the tower. They would need her. We quickly settled our bill and went our separate ways. My first instinct was to get to work, but when

I reached the train station on Seventh Avenue, it was cordoned off. The subways had been shut down.

I walked quickly back home, a little more than ten blocks. My neighborhood, usually busy and chatty even by Brooklyn standards, was silent. But what could we say? There were no words, just this alien speechlessness. Yet we could not stop looking at one another, looking right into each other's eyes. As I walked, I kept thinking of a passage from the lamentations of Jeremiah: *How doth the city sit solitary, that was full of people! how is she become as a widow! she that was great among the nations, and princess among the provinces, how is she become tributary!*

By the time I got home, the south tower had also been hit. I called my office. No one was there. It was close to the World Trade Center, and any of my colleagues who might have headed to work early, on trains that stopped at Cortlandt Street, in subway stations right below the towers, might have . . . who knew? It was still unclear how many were injured, how many had died. Frank and I watched, stunned. His instinctive response to this terrible event was to cook. It relaxed him and gave him a sense of purpose. In the afternoon, he got to work roasting a chicken, mashing potatoes, cranking out comfort food. E-mails came in from friends in California, Ireland, everywhere. Later on, my boss managed to get in touch and let me know that everyone from work was okay, but we wouldn't be able to get back into the office for at least a week. Lower Manhattan was no-go, inaccessible to all but police and emergency services and other essential personnel.

I called a college friend who also lived in the neighborhood, and asked if she wanted to come over. Who would want to be alone on such a day? She joined us, we watched the news, we ate, then headed to evening services at a progressive church just blocks away. It felt right and safe and necessary to be in a house of worship, to grieve collectively. But already the discourse of 9/11 started to worry me. The minister came uncomfortably close, to my mind, anyway, to blaming Israel for what had happened, which was not only premature of her, but facile. And besides that, it seemed counterintuitive and potentially dangerous for a pastor to do anything that might widen the gap between people of different faiths at such a time. Once again, mainstream church would not give me what I needed, especially now. But we stayed out the disappointing service, then went immediately to the nearest bar—a gay bar two blocks away. We saw familiar neighborhood faces there and had whiskey and greeted one another like survivors. The atmosphere was surreal, even if the sentiment in the room was both sweet and disconcertingly survivalist: *The city is burning. But we can drink. We can dance. We can love.*

The next day, I signed up with the Red Cross. I'd do whatever needed to be done—but I mentioned that I was preparing for ordination and would most like to volunteer on the spiritual care track, if that was possible. "Can you make a spreadsheet?" the volunteer coordinator asked me. The truth is, I was—and am—terrible at spreadsheets. But sure I could. Fine. If that's what they needed. "We got all these pastors coming in from all over the place. Somebody better keep track of them."

I was sent down to the Family Assistance Center, located first at the armory on Lexington and 26th Street. Chrissie, a cheerful college student—a proud member of Campus Crusade for Christ—and a Promise Keeper from Oregon named George and I were given a table and a stack of forms to go through. We made packets for the emergency volunteer chaplain trainings. If those two had any idea what my beliefs were—and I did make a halfhearted attempt to explain, but we had work to do, and it's not easy to explain—they probably would've been pretty sure I was going to hell. But we worked well and efficiently together, got along fine. At home that night I got a start on my visiting emergency chaplain database, and then showed up at the FAC the next morning. My first supervisor was a no-nonsense woman from the Midwest with years of experience ministering to victims of plane crashes and their families. She told me to go to the emergency chaplain training, even if I wasn't ordained yet. At least that way I'd get to meet a lot of the visiting volunteers, get their names, and start making schedules.

A group of more than a dozen Baptist pastors from Oklahoma had been sent to New York by the Lord to minister to its people for three days. That was all fine and good. I understood that even the Lord recognized that people do have jobs and families. But it was up to me to explain to them why, with a limited number of chaplains working the floor of the FAC on each shift, twelve of them could *not* be evangelical Baptist preachers from Oklahoma.

"Ma'am, we understand that everyone wants to serve. But we'd really like to be *together*," one of them told me, baseball cap in hand, pressed close to his heart.

It wasn't just that I needed to fit in everyone who wanted—and was qualified—to serve. "The thing is, it takes a lot to scare New Yorkers," I explained. "What happened a couple days ago scared us. And you know what else would scare us? A dozen Baptists from Oklahoma coming at us all at once."

I'll never be sure that he got what I meant. But there had to be a mix—Christian clergy of various denominations, imams, rabbis—and no one might seem as foreign to New Yorkers than him and his colleagues, no matter the goodness of their intentions, which I did not doubt. The chaplains on the floor had to at least come close to reflecting the diversity of the people affected by the disaster who might want their services. And what a crew we had: the imposing long-bearded, black-robed Romanian Orthodox priest, the gruff joke-telling Bronx rabbi, the earnest young liberal seminarians from Union, the gentle and genial Jesuit pacifist, Protestants of mainline and charismatic persuasions. But the Red

Cross instructions were simple and smart: *Be here for these people, listen to them, do your best to comfort them.* This was no time to argue doctrine or politics. This was no time to give answers, for there were none to give. This was no time to tell a mourning mother that her beloved son's death was part of God's plan, even if you believed that, which I sure didn't. Don't push. Don't preach. Pray with them only if they ask. Make yourself available. Show up. Be present.

The praying part aside, it's not so different, really, from how one should behave in a bar, no matter what kind of bar it is. And in the days after 9/11, the Fish Bar was exactly the kind of bar I needed. No pushing, no preaching—like a family, really, but a calmer and kinder family than many of us join when we are born. After the shock of the first few days, we spoke little of the event itself, using our time together to try to relax as much as we could, to talk about the things we normally talked about. In the best of times, New York is a pretty chaotic place. Now, that chaos had multiplied—even if an eerie calm had settled on the surface. No one knew what would happen next, but some of us expected the worst. One morning on the B train, crossing the Manhattan Bridge about a week after the attack, the subway suddenly halted, there in the middle of the river, and the lights went out. My fellow straphangers and I looked at one another purposefully, and I am sure I was not alone in thinking the worst, that maybe another attack was happening, maybe to the subway system, maybe right here on our train. Nothing was certain. And when it jolted back into motion and the lights came back on, you could practically hear a great chorus of relief following the few anxious minutes of fear and resignation.

N ot long after the attack, the Family Assistance Center was moved from the armory to larger quarters in huge tents on the piers on the West Side. It was like a makeshift city: Dozens of booths had been set up to offer all kinds of assistance and services—financial, spiritual, medical, psychological—to victims and their families. There were resting areas, dining areas, volunteer masseurs and masseuses with tables set up behind curtains, volunteers with therapy dogs making the rounds. It was bigger and busier and harder to navigate than the armory space. After one of my first shifts over at the pier, I called Frank from the Times Square subway station to let him know I was wiped out and would be heading home instead of to the Fish Bar. That night, I needed sleep even more than I needed whiskey. And sleep in those days did not come easily.

"Maybe you should go to Lenox Hill instead," he said tentatively, then continued, telling me that something was wrong and my father was very sick. He had gone into the hospital just after 9/11 for hip replacement surgery. He'd had the other hip operated on a few years earlier; that had gone well, making it possible for him to play golf and stay active and get on with it. This was supposed to be pretty routine surgery. I hadn't even bothered to check on how he was doing—partly because I expected it to play out exactly as his previous hip replacement had, and partly, I admit, because I was pissed off at him.

After the attack, he hadn't called to see if I was okay. It sounds miserably petty to me now, but back then it seemed to me that the natural order of things was for the parent to make sure that the child—even if the child in question was thirty—was alive and well, not the other way around. But 9/11 came in the midst of one of our not-speaking-to-each-other jags, the circumstances around which I do not even remember, but were probably no different from the causes of any of our other estranged and angry spells: There had been a misunderstanding, there had been an argument, we just kind of didn't get each other, and I think that caused us both a lot more pain than we were able to deal with, and it sucked, and so we'd just steer clear of each other for a time. Our timing, in this case, was spectacularly bad.

I went to the hospital. My father was in intensive care, hooked up by tubes to numerous machines, able to speak, but uneasily. I sat beside him and held his hand. Very slowly, he said, almost laughing, "Maybe this is what we needed to bring us together." And I told him I loved him, which, until then, had never been easy to say. And it was true.

For a spell life looked like this: I'd put in a few hours of work as a community organizer, a few more at the Red Cross Family Assistance Center, a few more at Lenox Hill Hospital where my father lay dying, and then at night, when all of that was done, I'd meet Frank down at the Fish Bar, to drink and decompress, to be someplace where no demands were made of me, where the grieving and the sick, the sad, the inconsolable, the shocked, and the angry existed on the other side of the door. That was the way it was, every day, every night. For something like three months, I could not have gotten more than five hours of sleep a night. If that. Did I sleep at all? I do not recall that I did. Looking back, I barely remember even *thinking* during all that time. It was all going, all doing.

And then, it was drinking. And I knew that at the Fish Bar, I had a place where people weren't just pouring me Jameson after Jameson, where I wasn't just a person who drank. I was a friend, and they were my friends. I knew that the people there—the owners, the bar staff, the other regulars—had, like me, lived through 9/11. We had been there. We had been together in this. We had shared in that singular experience. We got it, and had no need to explain or even, most of the time, say anything. I can't imagine a place that would have been a greater, more reliable, more consistent comfort than the Fish Bar was to me at that time. Never had I *needed* a bar more. It was stable. It was my anchor.

I also knew that they knew me well enough, and knew Frank well enough, that they were aware of and cared about what was going on with my dad. They'd ask questions but never push too hard. And those among them who were inclined to pray told me that they were saying prayers for my dad, and for me, and I was grateful for that, too.

Of course we drink for solace, we drink for comfort, and the drink does its job; it is a calmative and helpmate. But you can drink *anywhere*. You can drink at home. A bar gives you more than drink alone. It gives you the presence of others; it gives you relief from isolation. When you are a regular, it gives you community, too. And at the Fish Bar, it was a community with whom I could feel sad and overwhelmed and worried and know that I didn't have to pretend to be anything else. They were with me. As soon as I entered the bar, not only would Frank be there, but Paul, too, with a big smile and a big hello, and everything would at least be a little bit okay for a few hours, until it started all over again.

If you've ever read reviews of the Fish Bar on nightlife websites, it might not square with my impressions of it. This quirky, homey, good-natured little place I loved is regarded by many, it seems, as a total dive. I certainly never thought of it that way. And it's not that I have anything against dives— I've always had a soft spot for Milano's, the Subway Inn, and the Blue & Gold, three New York institutions that could hardly be divier—but I think that where the Fish Bar is concerned, the label's just not right.

The taxonomy of bars is extensive, and not without complexity and crossover. Is a dive bar the same as an old-man bar? No, not exactly, though old hard-drinking men can be found at dives. Old-man bars are, well, generally full of old men, and anyone who is not part of the general demographic is instantly an outsider—even if the old guys in question are friendly, and they sometimes are. Is a corner bar the same thing as a neighborhood bar? In many cases, yes, but the crossroads location offered by a corner bar is likelier to attract people from outside the immediate area than a bar tucked discreetly away on a side street. Among sports bars, there are those that cater to general fans or to those exclusively of soccer or basketball or baseball or boxing, to locals or expats, to quieter fans or *really really loud* ones, those located right near stadiums and ballparks and arenas that cater exclusively to supporters of single teams. And among gay bars, yet more expressions of all these categories can be observed—with a few extra subsets. Hotel bars are in a special category; when I want to drink in total anonymity right here in my own hometown, that's where I like to be, and when I travel, that's where I generally wind up after dinner by default. And even among hotel bars, beyond the generic could-be-anywhere places found in countless hostelries in innumerable cities and towns, other significant differences exist: There are timelessly elegant places like the peerless Bemelmans Bar at the Carlyle in New York and the divine jewel box that is the Blue Bar at Vienna's legendary Sacher and the little bourbon paradise at Louisville's Seelbach that belong in one category, and sleek loud caverns with thumping techno music in newer hotels in another. Obviously I love the former and would just as soon that the latter didn't exist at all.

Dives must have a mix—maybe one person who looks like serious trouble (even if he or she turns out to be a living saint), a few real down-and-outers of any age, usually at least *someone* actively on the make, a nervous underage drinker or two hoping to pass for grown-up or squeak by anyway, bemused regulars of various kinds—the comedian, the one who's seen it all, the watcher, the talker, the bore. And even if the Fish Bar has been host to exactly this mix on some occasions, it is neither dark nor dingy enough to count, truly, as a dive. Its bathroom can be relied on to be clean and stocked with toilet paper. It's hard to imagine fights breaking out there—though it's possible they have; it is a bar in the East Village after all—because the place is really just too good-natured and well-meaning for that shit.

For someone who has a hard time with authority, I never once questioned the demands the Red Cross made of me. I did as I was told, confident that they knew better than I did how I might be most useful. My spreadsheet worked out fine; I'd turned out to be a pretty damn good chaplain scheduler. When the logistics had been worked out, all necessary schedules implemented and paperwork filed, my second supervisor—the social-justice Jesuit priest from the Upper West Side, for by then the air-disaster specialist from the Midwest had been called back to serve elsewhere—pulled me aside.

"You ready?" he asked.

"For what?"

"To do this," he said. "To be a chaplain."

I'd been through the training and received my certificate. I'd seen many seasoned chaplains in action. I'd seen some of them do work that was downright brilliant. I'd seen others make thoughtless mistakes that made me cringe. In just a few weeks, I'd gotten a chaplaincy education unlike any other, a trial by fire. But I did not expect that I would actually be allowed to serve in this way.

"You know I'm not ordained yet," I told him.

"That doesn't matter. I think you're ready," he said. "And I think you'll be great."

He handed me a Red Cross chaplain smock, and I pulled it on. Holding hands, we prayed together, and he sent me out on the floor of the Family Assistance Center. I walked the many aisles of its sprawling labyrinth, where anyone who wanted to talk to a chaplain would see my Red Cross getup and flag me down. After I'd made the circuit once, a woman in one of the sitting areas waved me over. She was crying. I pulled a box of Kleenex off a table and sat down beside her. I held her hand. She didn't want to talk. She just needed to cry, but not alone.

About a week later, the Jesuit flagged me over again and asked how things were going. Fine, I told him, which was true as far as my chaplaincy work was concerned, but not the whole story. He had no idea about my father's illness, and I didn't want to go into it. I hadn't quite realized yet that these two dramas, my father's illness and 9/11 and its immediate aftermath, were, in my mind, becoming completely conflated, different aspects of the same event, two halves of the same season of despair. By then, my father had been diagnosed with acute respiratory distress syndrome and was drugged into something that resembled a coma. He was not unconscious, but he was unable to speak, dependent on the medical technology to which he had been hooked up. It seemed possible that he might recover, likelier that he would not. No one could say for sure. We could only hope for the best. I sat by his bedside most evenings and read to him, Tolstoy, the stories "Master and Man" and *The Kreutzer Sonata*. I wondered if, under the circumstances, these were too heavy. They felt right for the season, appropriate to the gravitas both in the city's streets and in his small intensive-care room.

"Good," my supervisor said. "I'm putting you on the next boat."

I hadn't been on one of the boats before, but I'd talked to many chaplains who had. No single action assigned to the spiritual care team was more daunting. These were the boats that took family members—many of whom had traveled from far away—on a short but agonizing ride down the Hudson River to the World Trade Center site. When the boat docked downtown, we'd have a short time to escort family members to the site, where rescue workers were still active, no longer hopeful that any living people might be found, but still searching for bones, for fragments, for evidence of the lives that had been lost there. I don't think anything has made me more nervous, or made me feel more humbled, in my whole life than accompanying people to the site.

On my first boat run, one victim's mother, who had traveled to New York from the Deep South, wept during the ride, and not long after we arrived at the site, she fainted. Confronted by her grief, by the force of its intensity, I felt useless. It was unlike any grieving I had witnessed before: It was vast, biblical. She keened. "My baby, my baby . . ." All I wanted to do was hold her, but there were other family members who shared this impulse, and they had far greater right to exercise it. I could only watch. I could only cry with them. We were issued masks to wear at the site to offer some protection from the toxic dust and smoke, but few of us could bear to put them on. Anything that might make us feel or look less than human was intolerable.

By December, the most intense period of Red Cross activ-
ity was winding down, and my father's health was wors-
ening. I was still living my life among the same five locations,
and always in the same sequence: I'd hit the office first, then
the FAC, then the hospital, then the Fish Bar, then finally
home for a few hours. But when I woke up on the morning of
December 21, something told me to forgo my routine and get
to the hospital immediately, before anything else. I'm no psychic, and I can't explain it, but I woke up that morning and
knew that it was the day my father would die. And that's what
happened, hours after I arrived at Lenox Hill. Surrounded
by five of his six children, his wife, some friends, unburdened
of the medical machinery that had effected little, it was over.
That he had made it through a grueling autumn and died
right on the winter solstice at first felt nearly poetic. But the
more I thought about it, the less meaningful it felt. It was not
a poem. It was not, I reminded myself, part of any kind of
plan. It was only death. And all the theology I'd read in the
preceding year, all the prayer, all the contemplation of God,
even the Red Cross chaplaincy, prepared me no better to
wrestle with questions of the soul, of an afterlife, of heaven,
much less to answer them. I had arrived at some kind of
peace in my relationship with my father, but only just barely.
There was so much more I longed to tell him.

There would be a funeral within days, and a larger memorial later on. There would be condolences from friends and coworkers and people I barely knew. In the weeks after a parent dies, there is much to do, so much to take in. It's a busy time. And you keep going and getting through it. And then, when you think that maybe the dust has settled and life will go on, out of nowhere, you get slammed, and everything just shuts down, and you're no longer sure if life really will go on. I'd spent more than two months trying to help other people cope with the plainly awful fact that people we love die, and sometimes in the worst, cruelest, most unthinkable ways. The only predictable thing about death is that it will happen; the only predictable thing about grieving is that it will be hard. There is no getting around it. And inevitably, for me, the events of 9/11 and the events leading to and surrounding my father's illness and hospitalization and death had become one huge, tangled, overwhelming knot of death and sadness and pain and love.

It is not uncommon, when one is mourning, to become physically ill. An angry rash broke out on my arms and across my abdomen. My breath was always short. My appetite disappeared—save for an intense craving for matzo ball soup from the Second Avenue Deli. Sleep was nearly impossible. Frank could not have been kinder or more patient through all of this, nor could my friends at the Fish Bar. But I retreated from everyone. Once the public rites of mourning have been performed, one is alone with one's loss. And I *needed* to be alone with it. I was in no mood for questions. When anyone saw how wretchedly sad I was, they assumed that my father and I must have been close, and I hated feeling like I had to explain that, no, we hadn't been, and maybe that made it a little worse, or maybe not, but maybe if he hadn't left the world at sixty-eight we would have someday been close, though I doubted it, but who could say? Some of the letters I received spoke of a person whom I felt I'd hardly known— not at his best, anyway, nor certainly at my best.

I quit my job at the anti-hunger organization and stayed away from the bar, from nearly everyone I knew, really. Even among people I loved and trusted, I couldn't socialize. I took some small comfort in prayer, but felt detached even from God. I can't imagine having gotten through the sad, busy, difficult autumn of 2001 without the Fish Bar and its congenial fellowship, but what I knew now was that bar culture— like everything else—had limits. It could not fix everything. Necessary as it was, and always had been, in mourning it offered little consolation. It was no match for my grief, which could only be enacted alone, and in private.

Springtime, and finally the worst of this long grieving was over. This in itself amazed me, because only weeks before I had not seen a way through it. And the city, too, was returning to something resembling its old pre-9/11 self. If anything, New Yorkers seemed a little gentler with one another, a little more patient. Our rhythm was still a bit off, anxiety lingered, our wounds were still fresh, but we were slowly pulling ourselves, and our lives, back together.

I celebrated my ordination at the Fish Bar with friends, family, and a few fellow seminarians. It was a raucous evening that might even have done the Muggletonians proud. It no longer seemed appropriate to organize a congregation at the bar, but I was promptly installed as Bar Chaplain. I wasn't sure if any bar had had in-house clergy before, but I was thrilled with my new office and took its duties seriously: Delivering a benediction on Saint David's Day, ministering to the populace when asked, even officiating at the wedding of one of Paul's brothers, right there in the bar. One of the bartenders made a little sign, Lucy Van Pelt style: on one side it said THE CHAPLAIN IS IN, and on the other THE CHAPLAIN IS OUT. And as soon as I walked through the door, when she was working, she'd flip it to the IN side.

Beyond the bar, I put my ministerial credentials to work officiating at weddings and same-sex unions to raise money for my favorite charities, and preaching from time to time at liberal churches with open pulpits. I wasn't sure what else I'd do now that I was legit, but my Red Cross experience showed me that you didn't need a house of worship in order to minister; that faith, if you were inclined to seek it out, or even just feel it, was everywhere in this city—even if it, too, answered few questions.

The Fish Bar is still around, still thriving, if a recent visit is any indicator. Since it opened in 2000, it became a beloved neighborhood fixture. I still stop by, maybe once or twice a year, when I have time to kill in the East Village. But my days as a solid regular there ended in 2003. Once again, I found myself drifting from a place that had mattered to me, that had been my local. That bar had helped me to weather— and to celebrate—significant hardships and milestones. My father's illness. 9/11. A good portion of the guests at my wedding in 2002 were people I knew from the Fish Bar. I had not always been successful in my search for meaning during those years, but I knew exactly what the Fish Bar meant: comfort and stability. It was never a platform for drunken excess or otherwise bad behavior. It was the only bar I'd ever shared fully with another person. It wasn't just *my* bar. It was my bar with Frank. It was our bar.

What made me drift away? In this case, the law. In March 2003, smoking was banned, by city ordinance, at bars in all five boroughs. But there was a loophole: Bars in which the staff consisted entirely of the owner-operators could continue to permit smoking. Knowing that much, if not most, of their clientele were smokers, John and Paul made the difficult

decision to be the bar's exclusive keepers. This made it, for a
short time—until the state law came down a few months
later and prohibited smoking in *all* bars, whether the owners
were the sole employees or not—one of the few places where
people could still smoke and drink in tandem to their hearts'
content, and they did. And it wasn't just the regulars. This
special, if short-lived, status drew in lots of new customers,
smokers one and all. I am a smoker, but still, this was too
much. I could no longer invite nonsmoking friends to join me
there for a drink. And inevitably, it changed the character of
the place—even when the Fish Bar had to capitulate to the
tougher state laws and ban smoking like everyone else.

In time, Paul left the bar business so he could go back
to school. Much as we loved John and many others who we
knew from the Fish Bar, it was Paul who had drawn us there
in the first place, whose presence and personality and friends
and family had done so much to set the companionable tone
of the place. Even if it would retain its sweetness and intimacy,
some things were bound to change with him out of the picture. Maybe, too, I was starting to accept the possibility that a
bar might not always be central to the way I lived my life, nor
to the ways in which I expressed my faith. That seemed possible. Possible, but not very likely. And a little scary.

9.

HEY, THAT'S NO WAY
TO SAY GOOD-BYE

Else's, Montreal

Early one morning in June 2006, I boarded an Amtrak train in New York City bound for Montreal. The long ride, more than ten hours up the Hudson Valley, along the Adirondacks and Lake Champlain, offered spectacular scenery—and gave me plenty of time to think. I had been invited to the wedding of a friend I hadn't seen in more than a decade. A musician and poet, he and I had been very close during my freshman year of college. When he abruptly left school—as I remember it, it was in the middle of the night, in the middle of the semester, and he never came back—I was blindsided, and my heart hurt. For nearly a year (and a year's an awfully long time when you're twenty) we'd been practically inseparable, and then, without so much as a good-bye, he was gone.

Frank had often heard me speak of this friend; he had some idea of how important he'd been to me, how much I missed him, and how frustrated I'd been in my unsuccessful efforts to reconnect. A brief e-mail exchange in 1999 or so just trailed off. So I was overjoyed to hear from him after so long, and touched that he wanted me to go to his wedding in Montreal, where he had lived for many years, where his fiancé grew up, and where gay marriage is not only legal but, refreshingly, regarded as no big deal.

Frank opted not to accompany me to the wedding. Money was tight, but it wasn't just about that: he understood how important this reunion was to me and felt that it would be best for me to go this one on my own, emotionally wound up as I was by the prospect of seeing my old friend after so many years. The wedding reception would hardly be the best time to catch up, but it might be my only chance.

There had been some big changes in the past year. Frank had started teaching at a college in rural Pennsylvania the previous fall, giving me more time by myself than I'd had in years. We both felt fortunate that he'd landed a tenure-track job that was a three-hour car or train ride from New York, because stable jobs in academia, especially in the humanities, weren't easy to come by. We knew other couples whose careers had forced them much farther apart than that: one partner in San Francisco, the other in New Orleans; one in New York, the other in a small town in Texas.

By comparison, our situation didn't seem so bad. As for me, burned out after nearly five years of antipoverty nonprofit work, I'd taken a job at a magazine less than a year before Frank started his new teaching position and didn't want to give it up too soon; my résumé was a messy jumble of non-profit and publishing stints, none of which I'd stayed at more than two years. I was thirty-five, and, professionally, it was time to pull my act together. Besides, I wasn't ready to leave New York for Amish country just yet. I figured I'd give it another year at the magazine, then take the plunge and set up house in Pennsylvania. We even looked at property out there, including a sprawling old brick farmhouse set in a lush vineyard. I started to think maybe I could live in the countryside, learn to garden and maybe even to make wine. I told myself that I could learn to love that life—but not just yet.

My experiences in California and Vermont had revealed that, as much as I love the woods and the mountains, I am a city person—more precisely, a New Yorker. I tried to envision myself in the country—not visiting, not spending weekends there, really *living* there—and couldn't quite conjure a credible picture of it. And sitting in the café car of the Amtrak train en route to Montreal, I was surprised by how excited I was to be on my way to a big city that wasn't New York, on my own for the first time since Frank and I had started dating. I made a long weekend of it, arriving in Montreal on Thursday night, two days before the wedding. I'd head home the Monday after the wedding. I'd only been to the sophisticated Canadian city once before, and that had been a long time ago, for a weekend in my twenties. I remembered thinking it felt almost like being in a European city, but also familiar and comfortable. I remembered the small mountain after which the city is named, and wishing I'd had time to climb it. Predictably my first visit had been taken up with tourist stuff: museums and sightseeing and a dinner of poutine, the beloved if grotesque local specialty consisting of French fries and cheese curds and gravy.

But on this visit, aside from detailed directions to the wedding venue and a list of restaurants recommended by a friend, I had little to guide me and nothing planned save the wedding itself. I hastily brushed up on my French, which was never very good to begin with, though I knew it wouldn't be difficult to get by with just English. Still, I wanted at least to try to speak to francophone Montrealers in something that resembled their own language. Rather than behaving like a tourist, I hoped to be a respectful guest in the city, mindful of linguistic preferences and local customs. Checking in to my hotel was no problem. Ordering dinner at a café down the street that night went smoothly. But as I sat at the bar eating my *bavette aux échalotes* and drinking a couple of glasses of Corbières, I couldn't catch on to the Quebecois conversation around me, much less join in. Still, I eavesdropped, picking up on little bits of information and gossip, enjoying the way the French was occasionally broken up by familiar English phrases. Full of steak and wine, I returned to my hotel, vowing that the next time I came to Montreal—and already I was certain there would be a next time, and that I wouldn't wait too long—I'd do a better job of practicing my French before I arrived.

The next morning I arose early to walk up Mount Royal, and then back down the mountain, through the heart of the city and into Old Montreal. Like New York, Montreal is a superb walkers' town, with vibrant pedestrian life at all hours. But its scale is more intimate and its pace slower; no one I saw seemed to be in any rush at all. I lingered through the warm, bright afternoon in the old city, walking its cobbled streets, stopping for a delicious lunch, sitting on a bench in a small square, watching the citizens of this seductive place going about their everyday business. Already, I had started to fantasize about what it might be like to live there.

That evening, after a quick nap, I freshened up and walked from the city center, where I was staying, past McGill University and through its student ghetto to the Plateau District to have dinner at a restaurant that a well-traveled friend had recommended. I had a map but hardly glanced at it, and instead of taking the shortest, straightest path, I zigzagged down small streets and across wide boulevards with only a vague idea of which way to go. I wound up on Rue Roy, eastbound, and when I looked at my watch and saw it was not yet six, I realized that I had grossly overestimated the distance between my hotel and the restaurant, allowing myself nearly an hour for a walk that takes about twenty minutes. The Plateau neighborhood, with its tree-lined streets and stone and brick row houses and small mom-and-pop shops, looked and felt much like my own in Brooklyn—but with a lot more French spoken.

The still-bright evening summer sun lit up the bright red geraniums in the wooden window boxes lining the royal blue façade of a bar at the next corner. Regulars—you can always tell who they are—were smoking and talking out front, and they looked like my kind of regulars. A wooden sign adorned with a sinewy troll and the word ELSE'S hung above the door. I could hear Lou Reed playing from the speakers inside— "Perfect Day"—and I knew right away that I had found my Montreal bar, though I had never heard of Else's. Instead, I had been drawn to it, as if by a magnet.

The smokers and I acknowledged each other with a nod and I entered the bar. It's not an especially small room, but a cozy one nonetheless, with green walls and wooden tables, an abundance of well-tended plants, and a piano in the back. I took a seat at the end of the bar nearest the door and ordered a glass of wine.

"Where am I?" I asked a guy sitting to my left.

"You're at Else's," he answered, as if to say, *Where else could you possibly be?*

"I know that! I saw the sign over the door. I mean, where? What are the cross streets?"

He pointed out the window to the street signs. I was at the corner of Roy and de Bullion. And then more questions came. Where was I from? What was I doing in Montreal? Did I like it? How did I find Else's?

I was from Brooklyn. I was in Montreal for an old friend's wedding. Yes, so far I liked Montreal very much.

And Else's, well, I just stumbled upon it. And I felt so lucky that I had.

Most of the conversation at Else's was in English, though French phrases wove in and out, and occasionally French overtook English and then was overtaken in turn, the two languages mingling easily and naturally. The bartender, a no-nonsense dark-haired beauty, was a filmmaker who had studied world religions at university. I had another glass of wine. More people came in. I mentioned to my new friends where I was going for dinner, and they nodded approvingly and recommended favorite dishes. One more glass. More than two hours after I had chanced upon this perfect place, I finally made it to the restaurant, where I took their suggestions.

Happily, the bar was on my route back to my hotel, so I stopped in for what was to be a cognac nightcap. It didn't work out that way. I stayed until late, drinking more cognac, meeting more regulars. It was easy to imagine being one of them: coming here after work—whatever that might be if I lived in Montreal—every day, living in the neighborhood, knowing all of them by name. The charm of the city, its energy and mix of people, had quickly made me a fan. But Else's sealed the deal: As long as there was a place where I knew I could be a regular—a bar I loved instantly—it really wasn't so hard to believe that I could live somewhere that wasn't New York. Maybe not small-town Pennsylvania. But Montreal? I could do this.

On my visit to the bar earlier that evening, I'd overlooked

the story of Else's that was printed on the menu. But later
that night, I read it closely:

> One day in 1993, a six-foot blond Norwegian named Else
> hailed a taxi in Toronto; five hours later, she arrived in
> Montreal. After years of living the quiet suburban life, Else
> was ready to return to her aquavit drinking, Rothmans
> smoking, Scandinavian fun-loving roots. At 50, she covered
> herself in tattoos, donned a pair of Doc Martens, unpacked
> her Norwegian trolls, and set up a shop in what is now the
> famous Else's on Roy.

There it was: evidence, a brief fable that confirmed my
powerful hunch that Montreal was exactly the kind of place
that lent itself to grand gestures of self-reinvention. If Else
could do it at fifty, couldn't I do it at thirty-five? I turned to
the guy next to me, the same one who had been there earlier.
"Is Else here?"

He nodded across the room to a portrait of her.

"In spirit," he said. She had died, he told me, not so many
years before I had happened upon her namesake bar. But her
image, and memory, still animated the place. I wanted to
know more about her, about how she lived and how she
died, but I did not ask him any more questions. Even without
knowing the details, her premature death did not fit easily
into the brand-new-life narrative I'd started constructing,
both for Else and for myself. I had the uneasy, even chilling

sense that, like all fables, maybe Else's had a moral, too—and I didn't particularly want to hear it.

I turned my attention back to my cognac and to my drinking companions. Our discussion of Else was over, and we resumed our lighter talk about differences between Americans and Canadians. It was getting late, and I had a wedding—and not just any wedding—to get to earlyish the next day. I said good night to the regulars and the bartenders. When one of the guys offered to walk me back to my hotel, I declined. But I couldn't deny that it felt good to have been asked.

I almost felt sorry that the wedding was the next day. *Almost.*

I probably wouldn't be able to fit in a visit to Else's.

Saturday's weather wasn't ideal for a wedding—muggy, overcast, a little rainy—but it turned out to be a beautiful event nonetheless. The location was an old stone house in a nature preserve at the edge of the city. The atmosphere was intimate and warm. A handful of far-flung college friends was there—Sam from Boston, Matthew from Boulder, Mark from Los Angeles—and I did get my chance to spend at least a few quiet minutes in conversation with the man I'd gone to see, my long-lost friend, one of the two handsome grooms.

After the ceremony, but before the reception was in full swing, he pulled me away and swept me off into a side room.

"I know we'll barely have a chance to talk," he said, "but I'm so glad you're here." For a few moments we just kind of looked at each other and smiled. He looked great: less hair, sure, but otherwise he'd hardly changed.

"So tell me. About you," he continued. "Quickly."

Quickly! I knew he was being funny, and that he had other guests and a brand-new husband to attend to, but how could I fill him in quickly on the events of more than a decade? I hastily covered the essentials: my marriage, my new job, my volunteering, updates on college friends I still saw in New York . . .

Laughing, he cut me off and said, "Look at you. A married woman. With an office job." And then, raising his eyebrows dramatically, with something like comic horror, he added, "And an expensive haircut. You have become a *bourgeoise*."

Again, he was being funny. There was no malice in his tone, no harm intended, just honest surprise. Still, it stung. I didn't know how to respond; it was just as well that he had to go talk to other people. To be fair, the last time he had seen me I was a disheveled if not unkempt vegetarian college freshman with unruly hair, wearing frayed green Converse high-tops and too many layers of long colorful skirts and no makeup, a self-proclaimed revolutionary and enemy of The Man in his many insidious guises. And there I was, a thirty-something in a sober black dress and, yes, my friend was right, a good haircut, mascara and lipstick touched up, working a stable job, married for nearly four years to an English professor.

Although my friend had given up the cello and didn't write poetry as often as he had when we met, he had made a living for himself as an experimental vocalist and performance artist and teacher who traveled the world—the kind of work he'd been committed to all those years before. He was a real artist, living an artist's life, and thriving at it. I'd long since given up my long-held dreams of being a full-time poet/activist. Such a life no longer felt attainable or realistic.

And now I could not help wondering: Had I failed? Had I betrayed my friend, myself, The People, Poetry, Revolution, Art, Beauty, Love—all the things we'd talked about during walks through the Vermont woods and over bottles of cheap wine in our dorm rooms, back when we were young, which now felt like so long ago, not only distant in time but in sensibility? I clearly hadn't turned out as he had expected I would. Had I disappointed him? He was joking, but jokes are never just jokes. My hurt turned into defensive anger: Was there anything wrong with being a married, grown-up person—after all, he had just tied the knot, too—with earning a living, with having a life that was stable, maybe even normal? What was so bad about that? Nothing, I told myself. There was nothing wrong with any of that.

For a very long time, I hadn't seen it coming, either. In high school, my enthusiasm for a multitude of bad habits— drinking more than I could handle, tripping, chain-smoking, shirking responsibility, hitchhiking, etc.—led more than one friend to predict I wouldn't live to be twenty-five. Well, I'd managed to get there, plus a decade, so maybe I was ahead of the game. But I'd never been one of those girls who day-dreamed about her someday wedding, who longed for domestic married life, or really even gave such a life any thought at all. I knew, however, that such an existence could be more than fulfilling: Many decades into their marriage, my maternal grandparents—despite ups and downs about which I'd gleaned a few details over the years—still seemed to me to be very much in love, still great friends, still sweet and light-hearted and often adoring in their interactions.

Inevitably, though, the marriage I'd observed most closely was my parents'. I have no memories of them being happy though I am sure, in their first years together, they must have been. I only remember them fighting viciously and, it felt to me, constantly, before my father left when I was seven. I knew more about their drawn-out and painful divorce proceedings than I probably should have. I do not regard myself as a cynic in any way, but I doubt that my parents' history as a couple could not have influenced my perception and feelings about the institution of marriage. As for having children, I'd never been anything more than ambivalent—and, by my midthirties, my long ambivalence seemed like a good

sign that parenting probably wasn't for me. I loved Frank
deeply, and our wedding day was one of the happiest of my
life. We'd not only had lots of fun together, cooking and
entertaining and going to concerts and traveling, we'd also
seen our share of hard times—especially 9/11 and my father's
illness and death so soon after—and together we got through
them. I don't think I could have weathered them alone. We
got engaged a month after my dad died. Marriage seemed
like the right, sensible, grown-up response to all of it. There
was no proposal; we had a discussion about the matter,
agreed that after having been a couple for six years it was
time, and before about 175 of our nearest and dearest, pro-
cessed down the aisle to "Our Love Is Here to Stay."

It also occurred to me that I was so affected by what my
friend had said because he had, inadvertently, touched a very
tender nerve. When Frank first took the job in Pennsylvania,
I expected to be terribly lonely when I was in New York without him. We'd been together for so long. I'd become accustomed to being part of a couple. And at first, I *was* lonely and
hardly knew what to do with myself. But to my surprise—
and it really was a surprise, as I had not for a moment even
considered the possibility that this might happen—I started
to like being alone again. I felt miserably guilty about feeling
that way.

Our discussion made an impression on me, but I didn't
stay mad at my newlywed friend. Now it was his wedding
day, surely one of the happiest in *his* life. How could I be

angry on such an occasion? I was still thrilled that we had reunited, still grateful to have been invited, still happy to have been there. And he had done well; his husband could not have been more gracious, more easy to be with.

After many hours of eating and drinking and dancing and toasting, I was tired but happy when I returned to my hotel room, and called Frank to check in.

"So," he asked, "how was it?"

"Great," I answered, which was true, but maybe not exactly the whole truth. I told him how beautiful Montreal was, how much I knew he'd love it, too. I told him about the food I'd eaten, the people I'd met, my walk up the mountain, the lovely wedding. I did not tell him about Else's, or about the conversation with my friend. He had a conference paper to work on the next day and needed to sleep. We said good night. But I was restless. I had too much to think about.

Sunday morning was clear and sunny, and I walked once again to the Plateau for the post-wedding brunch, a cheery and chaotic affair, another chance to see the happy couple, another chance for more hugs, for more photos to be snapped and toasts to be made. Some of the wedding guests were going to Quebec City for the day and asked if I'd like to join them. It was tempting. But what I really wanted was to return to Else's, only a few blocks away. Besides, I had dinner plans that night with a couple I'd never met, who'd gone to McGill in the sixties with a good friend of mine in New York, the poet and editor I'd met at Puffy's when I was a graduate student.

After brunch I picked up a Sunday paper and repaired to the bar. In the early afternoon, light poured through the big windows and reminded me of happy afternoons spent at Liquor Store in TriBeCa years before. I saw a few familiar faces from my previous visits, and although I quickly busied myself with the crossword, a cigarette break outside led to a political conversation with a few regulars that we continued inside. By now, the bartender knew me by sight and greeted me warmly. I felt like I'd been going there forever.

A few hours later I returned to my hotel to get ready for another dinner out. I called my dining companions and they offered to pick me up and drive me to the restaurant, which turned out to be two blocks from Else's. Daniel and Kathleen—a couple in their fifties—were wonderful, interesting people, and treated me to a luxurious French dinner. We ate and drank and talked, and I told them about my reunion with my old friend, the wedding, and about this great bar I'd found. They offered me a lift back to the hotel after dinner. "But I have a feeling you're going back to Else's," Daniel said knowingly. He was right.

Sunday night at the bar was quiet and cozy. The bartender and I chatted for a while. From her, and from the few regulars seated near me at the bar, I found out more about Else, and quickly tried to put what I'd learned out of mind. Later,

I met a couple from the Quebec hinterlands—by then, they were quite drunk and very friendly—who loudly sang an old folk song in French and filled me in on what Quebec life was like beyond the city, deep in the country. Sometime around midnight I bade them, the bartender, the regulars, and Else's good night. My train left early the next morning—and I was in for another long ride, back to New York, to work, to Frank, to real life.

My last morning in Montreal, I checked out of my hotel and started somberly walking the few blocks to the station. And the closer I got, dragging my suitcase behind me, the more I wanted to turn around. The weekend had gone by too quickly, but it had also been so full. My old friend. The wedding. The mountain. The smoked meat and—it pains me to admit this—the better-than-New-York bagels.

And what I had enjoyed most was this: exploring a city that was new to me. Meeting new people. Drinking at a great bar. Being on my own. I could not say these things to my husband when we spoke on the phone. I wasn't sure if I could say them to him at all. I couldn't stand the thought of hurting his feelings. Would I have to? Would it be worse to withhold these things? Would it be better?

What exactly did I want, anyway?

I stopped at a corner and paused for a few minutes. Standing there, I really could imagine a whole new life for myself.

Maybe I'd stay here, I thought. Forever. I'd already made some friends. And I'd found the best bar. And maybe that was all I'd ever need. I could find a little apartment in one of those pretty brick row houses on the Plateau. (The rent in Montreal was much cheaper than in New York.) I would perfect my French. I could get some kind of job—nothing too serious, maybe even go back to bartending. I'd start to write poems again. Maybe I'd let my hair grow. Maybe I'd get a lot of tattoos, like Else. Maybe I'd fall in love again.

What had I done, landed in a Leonard Cohen song? I thought about my kind, quirky, smart, thoughtful husband. It would be completely crazy just to stay in Montreal. To end my marriage, just like that. That was no way to say good-bye.

And I reflected on what I'd heard the previous night, about Else. She had died in a fire in her apartment that was started, according to some accounts, by a cigarette she had neglected to extinguish fully before she passed out, drunk— a tragic ending to the otherwise inspiring story of the bar's founding. I was sorry I would never meet her. I reminded myself that no one's death is a lesson; no one's death is meant to teach us anything. It disgusted me to think even for a moment that anyone's life is a fable with a dreadful moral at the end. But even as I hated thinking what I was thinking, and refused to believe it, I couldn't shake the sickening feeling that maybe Else's story was somehow cautionary, and that what it was telling me was this: Self-reinvention has a cost, and it is high, and it is terrible.

The morning after I returned to New York, I headed to Pennsylvania. Frank had to be there to tie up some end-of-the-semester business. He was busy when I arrived, but we went out to an Italian restaurant for dinner that night. I was anxious, and there was no way he couldn't sense it. I drank a glass of Chianti too quickly and immediately ordered another. I poked at the Caesar salad we were sharing with my fork.

We usually spoke to each other so easily, so fluidly. The tension felt alien. I think we both knew that, since he'd started working in Pennsylvania, we had slowly started growing apart, even though we talked at least twice a day when we weren't together. Distance has a way of creating distance. I tried to break the ice by asking him how his day had gone. He was too perceptive for that. He'd had a few boring meetings, he reported, but never mind that: He knew something else was on my mind.

"Something happened in Montreal," I blurted out. As soon as I said it, I was sure that he thought I meant I had slept with someone else, or done something equally fleeting and dramatic. He said nothing, and I continued. "I don't know what you're thinking. But I don't think it's what you're thinking." What I needed to tell him was even harder to explain.

So I told him about the talk I'd had with my old friend at the wedding, and about how the conversation had made me feel: sad, then angry, then confused and no longer at all certain about what I wanted. I also told Frank that I loved him, and that none of this had anything to do with anything he had said, with anything he had or had not done. This was on me. But what I had learned, I told him, was that maybe I needed to be alone, at least for a little while. Maybe we should see a marriage counselor. Maybe we needed a break from each other. I waited for him to say something, and it felt like a very long time before he spoke.

"I am so hurt," he finally said, "that I can't talk about it."

It took nearly a year until he was ready—a hard and tense year for both of us, but it could not be rushed. The following summer, we went into counseling.

Six months later, we separated.

I never did move to Montreal, but I returned for a week in the summer of 2009. It was as hospitable and appealing as I'd remembered, but as the site of such a difficult reckoning, I was frequently overcome by sadness. I rented a room around the corner from Else's and spent many hours every night there. I loved the bar just as much as I had when I first stumbled upon it. Some of the same regulars and the same bartender I'd met in 2006 were still there, and I was glad to see them. Although her picture still hung on the wall, Else's presence no longer loomed as large as it had three years earlier. Now I wanted to know more—not just about her, but about how the people in her community remembered and thought about her. Some of the regulars spoke of her with reverence and affection; others shrugged their shoulders and dismissed her as a drunk, as though her premature death had been inevitable. A candle is always lit for her in a candle-holder bearing her name on the bar—reminding me, as if I needed to be reminded, of how the choices we make, our best decisions and our worst, change not only our own lives, but the lives of those who know and love us.

10.

DRINKING WITH MEN

Good World Bar and Grill, New York City

Good World Bar and Grill existed on the fringe of the respectable world, at the bottom of Orchard Street where it backs into Division Street. In 2005, this may have been one of the last authentically seedy stretches of Manhattan: nowhere, a gray crossroads where the Devil himself may just be waiting to strike a deal. It is a nameless borderland between the discount fabric shops and handbag hawkers and old-lady lingerie emporia and other vestigial outposts of *Yiddishkeit* and the newer hipster hangouts of the Lower East Side and the noisy restaurants, fetid gambling parlors, and storefronts full of cheap dry goods of Chinatown. And from the fall of 2005 until April 1, 2009, this was my drinking territory. Two or three or maybe four evenings a week—plus, religiously, Sunday afternoons—I'd get off the F train at the East Broadway stop, get on the escalator (when it was working), exit near Seward Park, turn the corner, and walk just a little more than a block to Good World.

The place, owned and operated by a Swedish woman and

her English husband, had been around since 1999, but before I became a regular, I'd only gone there once or twice. It was a good-looking place: spare and handsome, all washed-out wood and tall windows and iron, with a little patch of yard out back, little more than an alley, really, but with some trees here and flowers there, a few picnic tables and benches. Inside, there was little adornment save for a massive caribou head mounted above the bar, but not centered, off-center, like pretty much everything else in the place. The bar-stools were notoriously and precariously high; the wooden floors pocked and scuffed but with jagged apertures here and there, like little mouths of hell, wounded and patched then rewounded and repatched, in which a heel might catch and make a visiting Eastern European glamour girl in stilet-tos let out a high-pitched squeal of terror—or a regular crack a predictable joke about filing a lawsuit.

For a time, Good World had plenty of downtown cachet— designers and art-world darlings and would-be rock stars and long blond Scandinavians wanting fixes of herring and meatballs and aquavit, and glittery European types who only appeared, in accordance with their custom, late late at night or early early in the morning. In its first several years of exis-tence, it had buzz. It was trendy. Which is probably why it never struck me as the kind of place I'd turn into a second home.

But in 2005, when my husband started a tenure-track teaching job in Pennsylvania, I was ready to be a regular *somewhere* again. Something internal had overtaken me: With Frank living and teaching in Amish country, I quickly reverted to the way I'd lived when we had started dating, without having made anything that felt like a conscious decision about the matter. I'd even started smoking again. He and I had quit together, but I figured it might be okay to smoke a few cigs now and then. And I'd never stopped drinking, but I'd slowed it down—wine with dinner was more my speed than whiskey after whiskey. I was older. I was married; less and less of my social life happened in bars. I was working as an editor for a magazine with a feel-good, quasi-religious mission, but a better job description—and the one I always used when people I'd just met asked me that tiresome question, *What do you do?*—was Inspirational Ghostwriter.

My daily work consisted largely of rewriting stories of spiritual uplift. The turning points in these stories almost always came when the narrator had hit rock bottom: a spouse had died, a wayward child's addiction had taken hold, a marriage was in crisis, a business had fallen apart, a family farm had been eaten whole by a twister. And then something— *something*—came into the narrator's life that turned it all around: a sickly foster dog, a tattered old heirloom Bible that had long been lost, some small sign or wonder. I liked my work; it was just kooky enough, like a combination of reportage and pastoral counseling. I liked my office; it was civilized and, at least compared to other places I'd worked, efficient. I liked my colleagues, who were kind and interesting. But for better or worse, the wholesomeness of my work, and the relative stability of my life, felt a little incongruous, like I was not quite myself. I wanted to feel like myself again. And even if I wasn't sure exactly what that might mean, I knew it would involve a bar.

I'd heard that after Liquor Store had closed, loosing a diaspora of regulars out into the city, many members of the old gang had wound up at Good World. Adam lived nearby; Luke had a studio within spitting distance. Others were willing to "commute" from TriBeCa and the Upper East Side and even Staten Island. So I figured that if I stopped by, the chances were good that I'd see some familiar faces. One fall evening in 2005, I left work in a fine mood, got on the F train, and headed downtown. Good World was conveniently situated just about halfway between my office and my Brooklyn apartment; it would be easy to have a drink or two there on the way home. I got off the train at East Broadway, the last stop in Manhattan, and was a little disoriented, not quite sure where to exit, until I felt a gentle tap on my shoulder and a soft, low voice speak my name.

"Rosie?" It was Henry, a dryly funny artist I'd been drinking with since my Puffy's days more than ten years earlier. "You going to the Good World?"

Yes, I told him, I was. But I couldn't quite remember how to get there. Even as a native New Yorker, I easily got turned around in this neighborhood of dead ends, doglegs, and angles that obeyed no ordered grid. "Follow me," he said. *Suivez-moi.* A call to drinks.

So far, this Good World business was working out. As soon as I got off the train, I already had a friend to lead me there and to drink with. And once we got to the bar, there were about a half-dozen guys I already knew. Some, like Ian, were only familiar by sight; we'd crossed paths at Liquor Store, where he became a regular just as I'd started mostly drinking elsewhere. Others, like Luke and Fritz, whom I was delighted to see again, had been regular drinking companions from years back. And still others, like Adam, by then solidly counted as friends, both in and out of the context of the bar.

That first evening at Good World, aside from Mariana, the sweet, stunning, splendidly tattooed bartender, I was the only woman at the bar. There was a lot of catching up to do, since I hadn't seen most of that crew in ages. The one or two drinks I planned to have after work turned into four or five, and I left around eight, agreeably buzzed as I got back on the F train. It had felt like a homecoming. It had been a good evening. I was happy to be seen, and to see.

Within just a few weeks, I was there about every other night. I became a regular so quickly, so effortlessly, it felt like I was filling a space that had been left open for me. But more than any other bar where I'd spent lots of time, Good World felt actively, powerfully, predominantly male. More than anywhere else, my femaleness stood out. "It's so nice to have a woman at the bar," Mariana said to me one evening, and one of the guys, who was sitting on the next stool, agreed. I told Mariana I'd try to bring more women in, balance the place out a bit.

I launched a campaign of sorts. One night, I asked my friend Alexandra to meet me there for a drink. She liked the place. Two evenings later, my friend Dina joined me. She liked it, too. When Ian walked in that night, he saw me and did a double take. "You're here almost as often as me," he said, laughing. *Not quite,* I thought. *Not yet.* The following weekend, I was sitting at the bar with another girlfriend. She, too, liked the place, the bartender, the lightness of the conversation, the ease with which everyone greeted everyone else, the uncomplicated fellowship.

But no matter how much any of my female friends enjoyed themselves at Good World, and they all did, none—not a one—seemed to have any desire to return the next night, or the next, or the next. Regularhood—the thing that interested me most, the thing I had craved and missed, the singular condition of bar culture that confers both comfort *and* privilege—held out to them no metaphysical allure, no sense of necessity. And this, I realized, set me apart as a woman who loves bars: the need to be known, to have a place of one's own, a place I could call *my bar.* Of course it was not my bar, not literally; it had owners; it was a business. But as a regular, one feels a sense of ownership; one is invested, if not financially, then in every other possible way.

One of the bartenders had christened the crew of late afternoon/early evening regulars—a mix of expat and American men mostly in their late forties to early sixties—the Golden Girls, after the popular eighties sitcom about a group of plucky old ladies living together in Florida. Some of the guys took it in good humor; others were decidedly not amused. I *was* amused, even though I acknowledged with faint unease that, though female and younger, I was considered a Golden Girl, too. I loved my fellow Golden Girls, who were always ready with stories and (generally dreadful) jokes, always ready to talk about music—there were those who only wanted to listen to jazz, those who never wanted to hear it, those who loved the Smiths, those who hated them, and invariably, all of the English expats sang along enthusiastically to Ian Dury—or politics or the day's news or any old BS that demanded a public airing in the safety of the bar. But there were many times I felt like the Margaret Dumont to their collective Groucho Marx. Now and again, if the conversation got a little too salty, a little too focused on a general or specific critique of female anatomy, I'd give a great dramatic eye roll and say, for example, "Oh, Ellis!" instead of "Mister Firefly!" And he'd cast his eyes downward, say, "Yeah, sorry," lightly slap his wrist, and tell himself, "*Behave now*, Ellis!"

And sometimes if they gossiped about an absent member of the group, I'd try to say *something* in the slandered party's defense, which can seem tedious and scolding and out of the spirit of the uncomplicated, everyday pleasure that we relied upon the bar to give us. (In this respect, Don Marquis was not far off the mark in *Her Foot Is on the Brass Rail*: "It is not the occasional rowdiness, the semioccasional bawdiness, of this barroom conversation which I chiefly regret. It is the philosophical admixture . . . spouted forth with the removal of all inhibitions. The very presence of a woman—any woman, any kind of woman—checks this.") Ellis told me more than once, "You keep us in line." Maybe so. But certainly not all the time. Increasingly, I behaved just as they did.

One night, my normally good-natured friend Ian—a musician turned graphic designer, the well-mannered, amiable, and exceedingly polite son of an RAF officer—delivered, after a bad day at work, an uncharacteristically foulmouthed tirade. His girlfriend, Laura, was not present. I was shocked. Even Ellis, not known for self-editing, was taken aback. "Man, you *never* talk like that, especially when there's a woman around," he said.

"Except me," I pointed out.

"*You* don't count," Ian shot back. "You're one of the lads."

One of the lads. Even if I already knew this, already knew that I was one of them, hearing it said out loud stunned me. It made me feel good, *and* it made me feel slightly queasy.

I was extremely comfortable among these men, but I wasn't sure I was totally comfortable with this not-counting business. Besides, if it was true that I really had become one of the lads, Ian shared in the responsibility for producing this condition, because, in me, he had created a monster. Of sorts.

Ian may seldom have cussed up a storm, but there was another language in which he was utterly fluent. Its lexicon included words like *fixtures, tables, results. Strikers, wingers, attacking midfielders. Offsides, fouls, corners. Arsenal, Liverpool, Aston Villa* . . . and, above all, *Tottenham Hotspur,* the undeniably charming name—with its pleasing consonance and satisfying glottal stop, its neat internal rhyme and arguably Shakespearean provenance—of the team he had loved and supported nearly all his life. Ian spoke the language of soccer, in the dialect of the English Premier League, and in this he was not alone at Good World. Adam had been devoted to Chelsea since his youth, and others had followed his enthusiastic lead, probably in hopes that doing so might make them equally cool. The bar did not have a television, but for important EPL matches, and for major international soccer events like the European and World Cups, a projection screen was hung from a back wall and the place filled up with fans.

I grew up in a family in which the *playing* of sports was by no means essential, but the culture of sport, its history and lore, was pervasive. My father was a sportswriter and

reporter, and although he and my mother separated when I
was seven, his vocation had left its mark on our family. Hundreds of hours of my childhood were spent at Shea Stadium
and Yankee Stadium and Madison Square Garden, usually
bored out of my mind. I've always had a soft spot for the
Winter Olympics, particularly the figure skating, but this is
not uncommon among women I know. And the single possession I treasure most is a photograph of me, at age three,
with Muhammad Ali. He is dressed in khakis and a pith
helmet—the picture was taken around the time of the Rum-
ble in the Jungle—and his formidable boxing-gloved hand
rests firmly atop my small head. My pudgy little-kid fists are
raised toward him, as though I could take him on. Perhaps
because of this photograph, and because of boxing's rich literary history, and because, I will admit, of its sheer theatri-
cal brutality, which I shamefully find irresistible, fights have
always been interesting to me, though I seldom watch them
anymore.

As for baseball, I was born and will die a Mets fan—
an allegiance dutifully served to my beloved maternal
grandfather—but I am an extraordinarily lazy and ignorant
one, whose grasp of the mechanics of the game will never be
better than tenuous. I got excited about hockey for a short
spell of two or three years, mostly during college, where the
Vermont climate seemed well suited to the enjoyment of the
game, and then abruptly stopped caring. For most of my life,

sports were never so much my thing—in part, I'm sure, to distinguish myself among my kin.

Resentment figured into my resistance, too. I blamed sports, to some extent, on my father's frequent absences even when my parents were still together; he often had to go to games, as it was part of his job. In my adolescence, I often made some money by transcribing his lengthy interviews with athletes. After typing up hours and hours of conversation with one savagely mind-numbing dullard, I complained bitterly to my father. He seized this as an opportunity to teach me a lesson about not stereotyping people and told me that the first time he met Jerry Kramer—the celebrated Green Bay Packer of Super Bowls I and II and not, I hasten to add, the subject of the interview in question—the strapping right guard was sitting on a bed in a motel room somewhere in America, reading a book of poems by Wallace Stevens. Well, *I* hadn't read Wallace Stevens yet and was duly impressed. My lesson was learned: Jocks are people, too, and sometimes they even read really hard poems.

Many years later, I was working on a project at my father's office. He was sifting through a big pile of his papers from the sixties and came across a note that made him blanch. He looked at me and said gravely, "There's something I have to tell you." I asked him what it was. He turned away from me and answered, "It wasn't Wallace Stevens. It was *Rod McKuen.*"

We never spoke of it again. I don't blame it on Rod McKuen—though I guess I could—but gridiron football would *never* do a thing for me. Soccer was another story. It probably didn't hurt that it is the sport in which the rest of my family seemed to have the least interest. Frank and I happened to be in France during the 1998 World Cup, and it was impossible not to share in the excitement of the people around us, not to get caught up in their collective *joie de football*. Evening after evening in a little Franco-Irish pub in the Loire Valley, we'd join the locals to watch the games. And as we continued our travels around Europe that summer, we watched matches as often as possible. I especially loved the Netherlands' national team, partly out of some sense of duty to my Dutch heritage, I suppose, but also because their style—even though it was by then little more than a shadow of the Total Football for which the Dutch had been famous in the 1960s and 70s—looked so intelligent and elegant, and when they lost to the indisputably great but far flashier Brazilian side in a penalty shootout in the semifinals, I was crushed.

Ian knew about my half-assed, fair-weather, World-Cup-centric interest in soccer. He also knew that I was at least nominally a Mets fan, and therefore predisposed to champion an underdog. To top it off he was certainly aware that I am Jewish, and Tottenham—for historical reasons about which there is considerable disagreement—has long been a team beloved of the Jews of north London and, by extension, elsewhere. This confluence of three key elements—*you seem to like soccer well enough anyway, you root for losers anyway, and you are a Jew anyway*—formed the heart of Ian's compelling case for my candidacy for Spurs fandom, which he launched in earnest in the fall of 2006. "Why don't you just come watch a match with us sometime?" he suggested gently and casually, not being a hard sell kind of guy. Okay, I agreed. Sure. Why not?

Let the record, an excited flurry of e-mails, show that I watched my first Tottenham Hotspur FC game on Sunday, November 19, 2006, a few days after I'd received this missive from Ian:

I'll be watching the Tottenham game at Central Bar. We'll be there for the 11 am kick-off. Come prepared to be disappointed, it's part of being a Spurs fan ("It's the hope that kills you, not the despair").

It was an unremarkable, uninspired, even a little bit ugly match against Blackburn, a team I have detested with nearly irrational fervor ever since. I brought a pen and the Sunday *New York Times Magazine* with me; in the event that my interest waned, I would at least have a crossword puzzle at hand. The game, played on a rain-soaked pitch, ended in a 1–1 draw. Ian's brow was tightly furrowed throughout, his focus intent. I was not exactly riveted, but for most of the ninety minutes of play, the crossword puzzle stayed in my bag. When we went outside to smoke after it had ended, Ian scrunched up his face and shrugged his shoulders. I got the message: This was how it was, being a Tottenham fan, and I couldn't say he hadn't warned me.

As I wish to remember the chain of events, despite this lousy first game, I returned, week after week, and gradually started to catch on, to get into it, to figure out who was who, who did what, who was good, who was not, to pick favorites (the suavely skillful and broodingly handsome Bulgarian striker Dimitar Berbatov) and not-favorites (the beleaguered and often hapless goalkeeper Paul Robinson, whose best seasons with the Spurs were by then over). In the version in which I prefer to remember how my love for Tottenham Hotspur took hold, what happened was that I persisted until, to my utter amazement, I was hooked, I was invested, I *cared*. I like to recall it as an experience of natural and incremental engagement, in which each game I watched deepened my commitment, no matter if it concluded with a win or a loss or a draw.

But the same e-mail record offers evidence that something quite different had actually been going on. It reveals that once the seed of the notion of the possibility of my becoming a Tottenham Hotspur supporter had been planted, it instantly took root. It is a fact that the first Spurs game I watched was the dismal one against Blackburn on the nineteenth of November in the year 2006. It is also a fact that a few days *before* this momentous and ultimately life-changing occasion, in an e-mail to a college friend and fellow New York Mets fan, I wrote, "After the letdown of the baseball season, I am devoting all of my sportsfan energy exclusively to Tottenham Hotspur." So it was *not* something as organic as I wanted to recall, but a deliberate and willful decision. It was, in its way, a lifestyle choice. I had made up my mind. I *wanted* to be a soccer fan, and, specifically, a Tottenham Hotspur fan.

Exactly what had brought on this ardent desire eludes me. Was it just that I craved something new with which to keep myself occupied? Was it that Ian's abundantly apparent joy in the game itself, and especially in his team, was truly infectious? Was it that, in soccer fandom, I recognized another means by which to effect my complete assimilation among the Golden Girls, to galvanize my place in the tribe, if that was in fact what I wanted to do? Probably all of the above. Still, the extent to which I came to care was, if not cause for amazement, surprisingly deep and consuming. It wasn't long at all before I was arranging my weekends around Tottenham games ("Sunday brunch? Okay. But it'll have to be after one-thirty.") and taking lunch late at work to catch the second half of the occasional game that aired on weekday afternoons at a pub near my office. In soccer, the game loved so intensely by so many people throughout so much of the world, I had found a sport that I, too, could love—a straightforward game with simple rules, thrilling speed, admirable efficiency, and many instances of beauty. And maybe *that* was all I'd wanted: a sport I could call my own, and a team I could call my own, after having spent most of my life as an outsider.

Ian was, and remains, the best soccer mentor a novice could have—never pushing too hard, gently offering counsel as necessary, pointing out pretty plays and great runs and spectacular saves without any disagreeable air of didacticism, and I believe that he considers me one of the resounding successes among his disciples. I threw myself into my soccer education with gusto, and sought out sources independent of his tutelage. I read books and blogs, watched classic clips on YouTube, diligently followed news of transfers and injuries, learned all the words to a number of Tottenham chants (which Ian, being as well-mannered as he is, rarely partakes of and often frowns upon, and which I would never dare to vocalize in his presence, save for the tame and frequent battle cry of COYS: *Come On You Spurs!*). Here is a personal favorite, a filthy and bellicose little number set to the tune of the English music-hall chestnut "My Old Man":

My old man said be an Arsenal fan.
I said, "Fuck off, bollocks, you're a cunt.
We took the North Bank in half a minute,
We took the Shed with Chelsea in it,
We hammered the Hammers,
With carving knives and spanners,
We taught the Millwall how to fight,

So I'll never be a Gunner,

Cos every cunt's a runner."

That's what I told my old man.

Though the major historic rival of Tottenham is clearly
Arsenal, its closest neighbor, I didn't instantly *hate* Arsenal;
in fact, I often admired the way they played and looked forward to their games against the Spurs. I came to consider
Chelsea the true villains of the league, adept but boring,
newly cash-rich, and deservedly cursed with the most irritating and hotheaded fans (excluding, of course, those few
among my friends). I reserved no particularly intense vitriol
for the juggernaut that is Manchester United, by far the most
favored team among American EPL fans. I hardly saw the
point in despising them, much less in supporting them. What
fun is a team that wins all the time? Where is the dramatic
tension, the possibility of being surprised by joy once in a
while amidst all the heartache? It seemed far too much like
being a Yankees fan, an altogether weak and unimaginative
proposition.

Ian's enthusiasm and pedagogy aside, I found Tottenham
Hotspur irresistibly lovable, and not just on account of the
team's adorable name or the downright poetic name of their
stadium (White Hart Lane, which I figured might just as well
have been the name of a spooky old folk song, or perhaps of
a Fairport Convention record full of spooky old folk songs),
their absurd crest (a cockerel, a flightless variety of fowl, *an*

immature male chicken, perched atop a soccer ball), and their endearing, promising, but frequently losing ways. They are known for playing in an attacking style, and aside from being a polite way of saying that their defense often blows, this means that they play assertive, often nervy, entertaining soccer.

I established some ground rules by which I still abide. I continue to say *soccer* far more often than *football*, for I can think of few species more irritating than American fans of the game who consider faux British affect an essential part of its enjoyment. They can have their Man United; they can have their Ben Sherman and Doc Marten costumes; they can have their Mockney BS and dismiss such-and-such defender as a *hopeless fucking geezer* to their poseur hearts' contents; I will stand by the Spurs and I will call the game I love *soccer*. I am an American, for God's sake, and nothing can change that. During games, I generally refrain from commentary unless there is something I absolutely must say, or unless it is late in the day and I have been drinking and can't help myself. Otherwise, I am content to watch, and listen, and learn. And, above all, to cheer.

But with time, I started owning, and giving voice to, no shortage of opinions. To the amusement of some of the Golden Girls, I started speaking of Tottenham as *we*. *We* desperately need a new goalkeeper. I hope *we* don't get rid of (then manager) Martin Jol, under whose leadership Tottenham had ascended higher than they had in years. *We* played a great game against United. Some of them sometimes laughed at me, and at least one patently, if tacitly, declined to discuss the matter with me at all, having deemed me, I suspect, an absolute arriviste and thereby an annoyance to one for whom soccer was virtually a birthright. (I cannot help but wonder if things might have been different if I had decided to support *his* team.) But I had the support and encouragement of many others, including our friendly and civilized little crew of Tottenham fans—Ian and Laura and T.J. and Arnold—and Ian carried on with his campaign with delicacy, forwarding links of particular import, alerting me to the heartwarming news that the Spurs were the most charitable team in the league, occasionally sending along agonized, soulfully Slavic headshots of Dimitar Berbatov, texting messages of delight or distress depending on how a given game was going. And when, a year or so after my initial embrace of Tottenham Hotspur FC, I took the subway into Manhattan to watch games less and less often, opting instead to watch at home or at bars in Brooklyn, nearer to home, and when the list of soccer teams I cared about and made it my business to follow expanded to include Ajax and Barcelona in addition to the Dutch National Team and Tottenham Hotspur, he accepted that the time had come for this fledgling to fly off on her own, fully and correctly confident that it would *always* be the Spurs I loved best.

There is a Dutch commercial for Amstel beer. In it, three men are chatting at one end of a bar. At the other end of the bar stands a tall blonde in a tight pink sweater. One of the men approaches her, all smiling and friendly. "Look, if the striker gets the ball between the keeper and the last defender," he asks, arranging three glasses by way of illustration, "what is it?"

"Offside," she answers without skipping a beat.

He thanks her and returns to his buddies, to whom he reports, grinning, *"It's a man."* They all have a good laugh.

Girls are not supposed to hang around in bars with men, and they are not supposed to care about, much less understand, the rules of soccer. I spent evening after evening at the bar with men, and now I passed many hours watching and thinking and learning about the game, immersing myself in it just as I had immersed myself for so long in bar culture. More often than not, I could hold my liquor just fine and match those men drink for drink. And now I could certainly explain the offside rule to anyone who cared to ask. "Football is all very well," Oscar Wilde said, "a good game for rough girls, but not for delicate boys." Well, I could live with being a rough girl. Or whatever sort of girl I'd become.

Tottenham Hotspur FC was the good and lasting thing that came into my life at Good World in the fall of 2006. But the same season also brought trouble.

It was early December. The holiday season was upon me, and I hated it. Late autumn, nearly winter, the cold busy span between Thanksgiving and Christmas: the time of year when, if I am going to drink way too much, if I am going to do anything colossally stupid, it's going to happen. I was anxious, the way I always am during the holiday season, and I had come to be especially anxious when my husband was soon to return to the city for a month's break, a whole month, after I'd been able to make my own schedule and do whatever the hell it was I wanted to do—mostly, sit on a teetering too-tall barstool at Good World, there beside the Golden Girls, my friends, the ones I was not married to, the ones I drank and joked and talked soccer with. Soon I'd have someone to be accountable to again, and I knew that my marriage had become a fragile thing.

It is cold cold cold but I go outside to smoke anyway. Soon one of my friends comes outside to smoke, too. He joins me in the dark vestibule in front of the graffitied doorway right next to the bar, and with two of us in that tiny space, it feels less cold. Still, it's windy, and he fumbles to light his cigarette; the matches keep going out. "Just light it off mine." That works. Now we're smoking. We're talking. We're laughing. And then we're kissing. I'd known him for a long time— more than a decade—without a single romantic thought about him ever having entered my head. But lately, over the course of a few months, he had been downright courtly. He had kissed my hand. He had praised my skin, or my dress, or my perfume. More than once, when I'd gone to the bar to settle my tab at the end of the night, I discovered that he'd already taken care of it. More than once, when I made motions to leave, he had accompanied me outside to put me safely in a taxi, opened the door, kissed my cheek, smiled, shut the door, waved. Much more than once, he had made eye contact and held it for longer than anyone else there, than any of these other men. Something was up, I was sure of it, and I didn't mind. Still, there in that dirty vestibule, I was surprised. And happy and nervous and guilty.

"I love you," he said. It's a thing some people can say with extraordinary ease—especially some men—when they have been drinking. "No you don't," I corrected him. But of course part of me wanted to believe it. And I knew that at that moment, my place there, there in that bar, there in that tiny little world that I loved and needed and had probably grown far too dependent upon, had changed. I also knew that all actions, even small ones, have consequences. And as the nature of those consequences started to settle into my gut, I knew, with a sinking and sickening feeling, that even if it would be a long, slow dying, as of that night, my life at Good World was over. It's the hope that kills you, not the despair. Any Tottenham fan could tell you that.

Code-switching, I have long believed, is the most valuable skill one can have in bar life, and it's something I've always been good at. I can quickly pick up on the way people speak to one another (formally? colloquially?) and adjust to it easily (probably because my usual speech is somewhere right between the two) and to what they're talking about (probably because I talk too much and like talking about nearly anything). It is not about being phony or grasping for the lowest common denominator, though I realize it may sound that way. It's about adapting—and about enjoying people's company not only on one's own terms, but on others'.

Because I can switch codes easily, I have felt comfortable, fearless even, in so many corner bars, so many pubs, so many dives. Because if you can talk, and if you can listen, and if it is easy and pleasurable to talk and listen to anyone, because you're happy to discuss anything, really, and to hear stories about anything, because you know that people *are* endlessly interesting and you know that they all have stories, and because liquor loosens tongues and you are paying attention and taking people seriously, you might just stand to learn something. Because at the bar it doesn't matter if you're an ironworker or a classics professor, a Trotskyite or a Reaganite, a Midwestern kid fresh out of college who moved to New York intent on making it as a rock star or some pickled old coot singing "The Rose of Tralee" into his whiskey. The bar is a leveler. Because as long as you can be here, *be present* as they like to say in therapeutic circles, be present in this bar, in this space, drinking and talking and listening, acting and reacting, you're good. But no matter how adept one is at code-switching, one still has a role; one is still, in some essential way, oneself. And my role at this bar was not Girl. My role was One of Them. And now that had changed. Now I was both, which made me feel like neither.

To step out of one's role is in itself a transgression, and it is possible that once you do it, bad things will happen. It occurred to me that, at Good World, being a woman among men had possibly already positioned me in a posture of transgression, that I had, in some way, enacted a piece of personal theater, a kind of extended drag performance, an aberration that might naturally lead to other aberrations. I thought of the American League playoffs in 1998, when, in the twelfth inning, the Yankees' Chuck Knoblauch, instead of finishing the play, got into a protracted argument with the umpire, standing there at first base, shouting and pointing, failing to pick up the ball lying within reach, while the Cleveland Indians runner kept going, circling the bases and tying the game, which the Yankees ultimately lost. The day after the game, in a graduate school seminar on Edmund Spenser, my professor talked about what had happened, using it as a way into a discussion of the character of the Redcrosse Knight in *The Faerie Queene*. What exactly had Knoblauch done? Well, among other things, he had stepped out of his role, my teacher said. He was supposed to be playing the game. He was supposed to retrieve the ball. Instead, he argued, and if you're gonna do that, you're supposed to wait until the play's finished. Arguing with the ump is part of the ballplayer's job, but it must be done in the right sequence. Knoblauch had upset the order, he had transgressed, and whether or not he had cost his team the game, his transgression had played a part in its loss. I had some idea of what I stood to lose from my own failure to continue performing my part correctly.

A week passed before I returned to the bar, and for me that was a long time. The next time I saw him—the longtime drinking comrade, now transformed into something else—he asked if I'd stayed away because I was avoiding him. "No," I said. "I've just been busy." But the truth is, yes, I was avoiding him, and also, no, I wasn't. I had been thinking. I had been wondering: *Did the rest of them know?* I wasn't sure. What would they think? Did I care what they thought? Yes, evidently I did. And I suspected that even though they were my friends, and even though they treated me so much like I was one of them, too much so sometimes, I wondered if they would judge me, because maybe, just maybe, the jig was up, and they knew, and I knew, that I really was *not* one of them after all. They were men; I was not. And as much as I'd come to behave like them, I was different. I was female; I was other-than-them. Because of this, fairly or not, I expected the worst.

If nothing else, I knew this would forever change the way I felt in that bar and among many of those people. I knew it could fuck it all up. (It kind of fucked it all up.) I had become deeply if quietly worried, and, worse, I was more than a little sad. In the end, I had lost a friend—for me, this was not just unusual, but an alien and alienating state of affairs—and forfeited the sense of ease, the enveloping comfort, that had made Good World feel like home.

After that winter, there were many evenings I'd get off the F train and start toward Good World, as though driven there by nothing but impulse, nothing but habit, maybe even something worse, something automatic, Pavlovian. Sometimes I'd slow down and think, *Why am I doing this?* And then I'd think, *I love* this place, but it pisses me off sometimes—a lot, even—and things have changed. *I'd think, I need to find a new bar.*

There's no shortage of places to drink in New York City. I tested out a few spots. I'd lately been seeking frequent refuge at another bar not far from Good World. Nice bartenders. Friendly regulars. But it just wasn't *my bar.* And Good World—by then the faintly funny irony of its name, at least as it applied to my experience there, did not escape me—was my bar, for good or ill, for both. Whenever I tried to cut back, to make myself scarce, to move on, something called me back. The peeling paint and weathered floorboards. The boundless generosity of the buybacks. The dark little side street. The bartenders who had become trusted friends, the barbacks, the manager, the waiters and waitresses, and certainly Annika, the owner, whose friendship I had come to treasure. The charm and inconsistency and singular eccentricity of the place. And not least the Golden Girls; even if one was now lost to me, they were still my brothers, my team, my tribe.

All of this proved too hard to give up. It wasn't time. Despite my ambivalence, I wasn't ready to go. Like some fucked-up Viking song of my imagining, the place kept calling me back. By then I was running a monthly reading series at the bar, and anyone who cared to know where I might be knew that they could find me there. In a word, I felt indentured. But if I could be loyal to an underperforming soccer team, I wanted to be loyal to Good World, too, even if it was quite possibly driving me crazy.

One Saturday in June 2007 had been extremely hot, and I'd had to work through the morning and afternoon at a crowded, airless convention center. By early evening I was tired and cranky and hadn't found time to eat, but I went to an art opening in Williamsburg anyway, got roaring drunk, danced, got stoned, drank some more, danced some more, then proceeded to Good World to drink yet some more. I continued until the early morning hours, and then, perhaps inevitably, melted down. I sat in the little garden out back and bawled my eyes out in the company of people with whom I drank nearly every night, but who had *never* seen me cry. I didn't go to the bar—any bar—to cry.

"What's gotten into you?" one of the Golden Girls asked

unhelpfully. I kept sobbing. Someone else tried to say something soothing. A few others backed away. I just cried louder and harder. I moved inside to the bar, where strangers looked at me either with as much sweet drunken pity as they could manage or with unmistakable disdain. I couldn't take it, not from friends, and certainly not from strangers. In its sheer ugliness, this thing had taken on an uncomfortably Grand Guignolesque aspect, and I felt slightly feral: I could maybe scratch their eyes out, or maybe just shout obscenities until I'd scared them senseless. But I couldn't; at least I was not *that* person, *that* drunk. Instead, I took leave of my glass of wine, the seventh or eighth or ninth of the night, exited the bar, and walked to the corner as fast as I could without falling down. A hot steamy day had turned into a thick damp night, and there were no vacant taxis to be seen. Two friends followed me outside to check on me and try to help me get a cab. "Fuck off," I barked. They fucked off.

So now I am a weeping woman alone on the corner of Allen and Canal at three A.M. or whatever time it was. I am running mascara. I am self-loathing despair. I am a spectacle.

Finally, after what feels like forever, a taxi pulls up and I get inside. I am still a complete wreck, but I do not fail to notice that the driver is exquisitely, wrenchingly handsome, like a prince in a Persian miniature painting, maybe, or a Bollywood matinee idol. He has a great luxurious pile of shiny black hair and a noble aquiline nose and lustrous, unblemished skin. His huge dark-brown eyes shimmer. He is a person of rare and disarming beauty. He is a vision. I believe he is an angel sent from heaven by God himself. I tell him my address—the tears and the snot have made it hard to enunciate, and I am sure I said *theventeenth thtreet*—and he turns toward the bridge.

"Miss?" he asks tenderly. "You are crying, miss?"

I sniffle and confirm that *yeth*, I am crying.

"What's wrong? What has made you sad?"

I have to think about that.

I could say too much booze, too much pot, not enough to eat, raging hormones, deep disappointment in myself and in some others, a powerful sense of personal failure, nagging troubles at home, at work, at *that bar*. It all seems too complicated to go into. "I don't know," I answer.

"Miss, what have you been doing this night?" he asks.

Good question. What *have* I been doing?

"I have been drinking with men."

There is a long pause. I can tell that he is not sure what to do with this information.

"And I think I'm tired of it," I add. I am not certain that I mean it, but I cannot stand the silence. I want to hear him speak. I want to talk.

"You'll be okay, miss," he says soothingly.

"Yeah, I'll be fine." I laugh a little.

"See?! *You're laughing!* That means you'll be okay."

I can find no fault with his reasoning. My tears slow

down, but my face is burning, stinging from all that salt. My breathing slows, too, and steadies; it had been labored and uneven while I wept. I roll down both of the back windows just a crack to let in some air, and sink deeper into the seat. The bridge is empty and slick, but I am comforted, not afraid. It feels like we are gliding across it, like we are gliding with easeful, effortless grace across the East River, away from Manhattan, away from the bar, away from my meltdown, away from everything I want to get far away from. Down below and off to the right, a thin but steady rain-dappled streak of cars on the stretch of the BQE under the Brooklyn Heights Promenade looks like the trail of a shooting star, until the express subway whooshes by and blocks my view. Then the Jehovah's Witness headquarters come into my line of vision. READ GOD'S WORD THE HOLY BIBLE DAILY, one of their buildings proclaims in giant block letters. *Tried that,* I think.

"Where are you from, miss?"

"Here," I tell him. "New York. Where are *you* from?"

"I am from Pakistan."

"Are you Pashtun?" I ask him, even though, drunk as I am, it registers that he is from Pakistan, not Afghanistan, and it is therefore unlikely that he is Pashtun, and I know that I have asked a dumb and perhaps impertinent question.

"No, no, I am not Pashtun." He laughs again. Now I am convinced that he has the most wonderful, open, honest laugh I have ever heard. "Why do you ask?"

I explain to him that I have come up with a plan. I explain

that I have figured out how to change my life, which is objectively not such a bad life at all, for I have not lost all perspective and I know at least that much, but with which I am nonetheless, at this time anyway, deeply unhappy.

"I have a book idea," I tell him. "I am going to move to Kabul, find an aging one-eyed Pashtun warlord, and become his difficult Jewish wife from Brooklyn. Maybe his sixth or seventh wife. I don't care! I think it's a *great* idea." I slip into a brief silent reverie, imagining the crazy clash-of-cultures sitcom that might be based on it, an *I Love Lucy* for our anxious post-9/11 age.

He laughs some more. That laughter; I could listen to it forever. But then it stops. "It's a great idea," he concedes. "But there is a problem." His voice is deeper now, and serious.

"What's the problem?" I ask.

"Your one-eyed Pashtun husband will cut off your hands before you are able to write this book." He shakes his head, turns to glance at me through the cracked plastic partition, and smiles.

Now I am laughing, hard. We are breezing briskly down Brooklyn's Fourth Avenue, and we are both laughing. I ask him to take a left just after the underpass, please. He turns onto my street and comes to a stop, with great care, in front of my building. I pull a crumpled twenty-dollar bill and a few singles out of my bag, smooth them out a little, and hand him the money. He hands it back. "Please," I implore him, "take it." He refuses.

"No, no, no," he insists. "I am on my way home anyway."

"You sure?" He says he is sure. I thank him. He laughs some more, and so do I.

"*See?* You're still laughing. You'll be okay, miss," he tells me again, then pauses. "You'll find a better way to change your life."

He does not drive away until he has seen me walk up the stoop and unlock my front door. I wave good-bye. He waves good-bye. I could not be more grateful. I could not love him more.

September 2008 brings big news, but there had been murmurings for months: Star striker Dimitar Berbatov is leaving Tottenham Hotspur and has signed with Manchester United. I am bereft. Ian is disappointed, but he takes it with his usual philosophic, let's-move-forward-then attitude. And there's other talk circulating at Good World. Rumors are rampant: The place is closing, and soon. Probably by the spring. The building has been bought; the upstairs tenants have been told to shove along. Many of the Golden Girls are resigned. We'd seen bars we loved come and go before; this was standard New York life-cycle stuff. We had moved on before. We could move on again.

By the time the rumors turn into cold hard fact, Annika seems terribly sad. This place was her baby. She is my friend.

I want her to be happy and successful, so I do not tell her that part of me welcomes the news, now that it is decisive, now that it is a done deal, although I wish it had come to pass under different, and better, circumstances. I had not been able to find a way to extricate myself from this bar, and forces beyond my control had made a way for me. It was a relief, but one not without attendant sadness.

I was relieved that Good World would not stagger and sputter haltingly to its death the way Liquor Store had. I object to the notion of closure, which always seems bogus and impossible, but maybe this would offer something resembling it. I was glad I would be there to witness the end-game, to watch it all shake out. It certainly would not be the first time I'd parted ways with a bar, but in this case I felt an invigorating and novel sense of agency: I could choose how to say farewell, in the best way I saw fit. There was an end date. There was lead time.

About a week before the bar was set to close, I knew what I had to do. I drafted an e-mail to most of the Golden Girls and a few other regulars. It read:

Dear friends,

"O brave new world, that has such people in't!" Some of you know that it has long been one of my crazy dreams to stage Shakespeare's *The Tempest* at Good World.

With Good World closing on 3/31, undertaking a full-on production with sets and costumes and the works won't be possible.

So what I'd like to do is gather a group of Good World folks together to sit around a table on Sunday at 2:00 to read the text aloud. We'll draw parts from a hat, but if there's a role you feel you were born to play, we can surely work something out.

"Few plays are so haunted by the passing of time as *The Tempest*," wrote the critic Northrop Frye. *The Tempest* was Shakespeare's last play, and is a work intimately concerned with endings and beginnings. As such, I hope it will be a sweet tribute to a place that has been like a second home to many of us.

Please let me know if you'd like to participate . . . I hope you're game: "As you from crimes would pardoned be/Let your indulgence set me free."

I attached a jpeg of J. W. Waterhouse's painting *Miranda* and hit send. A few days later, the Good World Shakespeare Company convened: it included Annika, Luke, Arnold, Fritz, Samuel and T.J. We drew our parts, written on little cards I'd folded and put in martini glasses, each taking one large role and one or two small ones. I was disappointed to get Miranda—it seemed like a minor cosmic joke that I, of all people, would get stuck as the ingénue—but I went with it.

Annika made a wild and brilliant and terrifying Caliban. Luke, our Prospero, marched through his many monologues and hundreds of lines with occasional exasperation but good cheer, and ad-libbed whenever he felt like it.

I am certain that no one enjoyed this as much as I did. My friends were doing me a favor, handing me the ending I wanted. But where else could this possibly happen? Who else would ever indulge me quite like this, that some spell I needed to be broken might really and finally break, and on my own terms? During a longish gap in which Miranda does not appear onstage, I stepped outside, smoked a cigarette, psyched myself up for the final act in which the stranded are rescued, the villains vanquished, the spirit set free, and looked in at these people, this funny troupe of players gathered around a table. They looked like a painting, like something from the nineteenth century, and in their faces and in the details—the bottles of beer from which any and all could drink, the packs of cigarettes strewn around for sharing, the bodies huddled a bit closely together for warmth—I saw, as though captured in a frame, the specialness of the place, the collective and communal spirit that had made me love it even when I didn't. To an outsider, this might have looked like the most slapdash, ridiculous, worst production of *The Tempest* ever staged. Shakespeare himself might have been turning in his grave, but I would not soon forget this great and gracious and generous gift, this indulgence my friends had given me. I certainly would never forget them.

Good World goes out with a bang: a closing party that starts on the last evening of March and ends the following morning, April Fool's Day. Most of the furniture has already been cleared out, many of the fixtures removed. For the first few hours, it's just a bunch of regulars and staff members (who had often seemed interchangeable), some friends of regulars and friends of friends of regulars, a few familiar hangers-on. It is quiet enough for conversation. There is milling around and chatting, and an air of mild melancholy, a pervasive strange sensation of nostalgia for the present. But by midnight the joint is jumping: There are bodies wall-to-wall, and it is a bash, a blowout, a bacchanal. A spread of bread and cheese and chicken legs has been set up in the back like a medieval feast tableau. Regulars from years earlier turn up. Curious passersby come in tentatively, then stay for hours. And everyone makes nice, no matter how they really feel about one another. Any grievances are, for now, suspended. We may all feel like ghosts now, but we are friendly ghosts.

Annika, resplendent in shiny silver leggings and a T-shirt that says, in tabloid-style lettering, MY BOOZE HELL, is swinging from the pipes suspended from the ceiling, a cigarette between her lips. There is dancing on the bar and on the banquettes. There is predictably a great deal of drinking. There is some crying, but not, as far as I can tell, the worst kind. There is a whole lot of kissing, in expected and unexpected combinations. There is some serious making out. There is a whole other party going on in the basement. There is more than one arrest.

This party, one friend remarks, feels like the old days—when New York was fun.

And this is absolutely as it should be. This is the way it must happen. I have dressed up for the occasion, out of respect, but at some point my polka-dot cocktail dress is mostly obscured by a capacious black-and-white Celtic FC hoodie I have acquired that night under somewhat shady circumstances, my hair is a mess, and I have stopped bothering with the reapplication of lipstick. And that's fine. This is home, and I could be wearing a trash bag for all anyone here would care. And this *is* fun, if a little surreal and charged with emotion. Some regulars leave earlier than I'd expected, not wanting to make such a big deal of it, because, I suspect, it really *is* a big deal. Others will stand their ground until the landlords come and kick them out, even long after every last drop of booze has been drained.

My friend Samuel staggers over to me. He has been drinking quite a lot, as we all have. He edges up close to me, a little too close, maybe, but that's his style. And Samuel, an artist, is a gentle man with a sweet soul, but his accent (English boarding school with occasional South American flourishes), his distinctive, unhurried speech pattern, and his deadpan delivery conspire to make him sound like he could convincingly play the part of a subtle, urbane, quietly crazy and exceptionally deadly villain in a British gangster movie. He eases an arm around my shoulder and, as is his unnerving custom, looks me right in the eyes. Samuel can go for a long time without blinking.

"I love you, Rosie," he says. "Do you know *why?*"

I shrug and say no, I do not know why, not exactly, anyway.

He stares a little harder and answers *very* slowly.

"Because you're like a guy," he says. "But you're *not.*"

EPILOGUE:
THERE IS ALWAYS
A STORY AT MILANO'S

New York City

After Good World closed, I was suddenly no longer a real regular anywhere, but set adrift in a city full of bars. The places where I'd occasionally sought refuge when the intrigues at Good World had gotten me down had, it turned out, been best suited for that. I didn't feel perfectly at home in any of them. They just weren't Good World. Or, for that matter, Liquor Store. Or the Fish Bar. Or the Puffy's I'd known and loved in the mid-1990s. Or Grogan's. They were fine bars, but they didn't feel quite right. Of course, there was no way I'd stop drinking in bars. That was unthinkable. But for a time I wandered—to places that had piqued my curiosity, to old standbys I'd not visited in ages, to the many new spots suddenly popping up closer to home, right in my Brooklyn neighborhood, where a bar boom was in full swing. Without a bar of my own, I felt a little bit lost. But, like Ariel at the end of *The Tempest*, I also felt surprisingly free. There was no longer anywhere in particular I had to be.

One Thursday night in October 2009, I went to a poetry reading in Manhattan, way uptown. It wound down around ten, and I left with much to think on, wide awake and a little thirsty. I got off the 6 train at Bleecker Street, figuring that a nightcap at Tom & Jerry's, a good, solid, reliable place, would be just the thing. But it was packed, and so, for the first time in probably fifteen years, I went to Milano's. What compelled me to do this I cannot say. Milano's is one of the last great dives in New York, but as the site of occasional debauchery in my early twenties, not a place I'd been much inclined to revisit as a grown-up.

It's super-narrow and tiny, Milano's. There aren't many seats at the bar. Most were taken, one had a briefcase on it signaling that it, too, was taken, and one was empty. I claimed the empty seat and ordered a Jameson. To my right sat a woman I'd met a couple times, a friend of some friends. We greeted each other cheerfully and caught up. I told the young Irish bartender—and right away I liked this bartender, a live one—how I *never* come to Milano's anymore, how it has been something like fifteen years, but here I am, after all this time, sitting next to someone who is not a stranger at all. She confirmed that it was an excellent thing and proceeded to turn up "Thunder Road" really loud and sing along: *"Show a little faith, there's magic in the night/You ain't a beauty, but hey, you're all right."* Maybe the best lyrics ever.

To my left sat a friendly and appealing man. He also agreed that this was a fine thing, this showing up here after such a long absence and seeing a familiar face. "When you came in," he told me, "you looked like you were looking for a friend," which I thought was the most wonderful and ambiguous thing to say. We clear up that he hadn't meant it in a you-looked-sad-and-desperate way. I told him he looked really familiar.

"International, maybe?" he asked.

"International?" I asked. "Are you some big internationally famous person I should recognize?" (He laughed; he'd meant from the bar the International on First Avenue, and I felt like a moron—though, to be fair, you just never know who might turn up at Milano's.) He got up to go to an ATM—Milano's is cash only—and asked me if I'd still be there when he got back. I had taken only a sip or two of my whiskey, so I said, yes, it is likely that I will be.

He returned and ordered us another round. "You know," he said, "*you* look really familiar, too." I told him my name.

"Rosie what?"

I told him my last name, too.

And suddenly it's all: *Oh. My. God.*

We used to drink together, pretty often, at another bar, in another borough, in another decade. We clinked glasses. We had not seen each other in more than ten years, and he reported that the last time we'd met was on a Long Island Rail Road station platform, completely by chance, just like this, but we had been headed to different destinations. I did not remember it, but I also did not doubt it. We reminisced about the old days—the ones we had in common, anyway. And I reported that in the intervening years, life had, if nothing else, been indisputably life-y. I briefed him on the milestones: my father's death, my marriage, Tottenham winning the Carling Cup in '08, this big lucky professional break I'd gotten, a loved one's illness. He filled me in on his previous decade: a marriage, a few years away from the city, work stuff, a divorce, a new marriage, his return to New York. A lot of life can happen in ten years.

He asked me if he might speak freely, and I told him I would want nothing less. So he said, "You know, back then, I always really liked you." And this was followed by a litany of flattering things that managed to sound entirely sincere. And I had always really liked him, too. He was, and is, lovely and gracious. But back then, of course, he had a girl. And I was someone else's girl.

A few moments of silence. We're both gazing into our glasses now, not looking at each other. I can't speak for him. I can't read his mind. But I, for one, was doing a little thinking of the *what-if* variety. So I ordered us another round. Another Jameson for me, another bourbon for him. He told me he could pay. "I know that," I said, "but I'd like to get this one, please." We drank some more. We talked some more. And, well, I felt a great chemical charge and wondered if in another lifetime we might have hastened to the grungy little bar bathroom, locked the door behind us, and ripped off all our clothes.

But more than that, better than that, there was just this comfort, this openness, this ineffable sweetness. Bruce Springsteen is right: there *is* magic in the night. It was just really nice, is what it was. And by then it seemed to me that we were quite madly in love, even though it was only a temporary affliction, the result of the heady combination of alcohol and attraction. And nostalgia. And this bar's own powerful mojo. (I know a woman and man who met here— she says she peeled him off the floor and dusted him off— and they have been a happy couple now nearly a score since. A former Milano's bartender told me about the long-ago afternoon when a regular, a burly court officer drunk and sugar-high after many rum-and-Cokes, pulled out a pistol and aimed it at the poker machine, shouting at it to give him back his money, until said bartender eighty-sixed him as coolly as he could manage. And I know another man who, in his youth, spent a night here so debased and distressing that he refused to utter a word about it more than twenty years later. There is always a story at Milano's.)

We were older now, my long-lost drinking companion and I. And possibly smarter. Whatever I wanted from bars when I first starting going to them, this is what I wanted now, and I couldn't imagine anything better. This connection. This empathy.

We got quiet again. He patted me on the back and smiled. I extended my hand, and we shook. We agreed that it was great to see each other again, there at Milano's of all places, where we never hung out, here, after all this time, out of nowhere. Sensibly, we finished up our drinks. We said good night. We wished each other well. And we left. Headed, once more, toward different destinations.

W here *was* I headed? At that moment: to Brooklyn, home, to my bed, to sleep.

In the grander sense, I didn't know for sure where I was going, but something that night had shifted. And of course it was that night, but it was not *only* that night. It was that year. It was the last few years. My work, my marriage, even my habits: All these had changed, in big ways and small, because of age, because of time, because of experience. Maybe I no longer needed to be a regular anywhere anymore, at least not the way I had been. A chance visit to a bar I seldom drank in had been so strangely meaningful, so rewarding. And I knew that if I'd just defaulted and gone to one of my usuals, it wouldn't have happened. One of the comforts of regularhood is that it holds few surprises; its rhythms are steady and consistent and predictable, so that when any disruptions occur, they are all the more jarring, and sometimes terrible, as they had been at Good World. Maybe I needed to take more chances with bars. Maybe I needed to be willing to be a stranger again.

One of the new places that was part of the bar boom in my neighborhood was especially inviting. It's a little place, with about ten seats at the bar, four booths that seat four

people each, and a yard in the back with enough space, on a
nice day, for about the same number of drinkers that fit
indoors. It's a mom-and-pop joint, run by a local couple—
mainly a beer-and-shots bar, nothing fancy or complicated
(though you can get an excellent Manhattan). One night, not
long after it opened, one of the owners asked me if I knew
anyone who was looking for a shift or two. I took it as a hint.
(I'm still not sure if she hoped I might be interested, but
that's how I interpreted the question.) I hadn't been on the
other side of a bar in more than fifteen years, and hadn't
given it even a minute's thought. But maybe it would be the
perfect way to break up a week that otherwise consisted
mainly of being home, alone, writing. I was starting to feel
isolated. I told her I couldn't possibly work nights—I felt far
too old to close a bar at four A.M.—but I wouldn't mind giving one day shift a week a shot. The next day, I was trained.
And I've been happily working there ever since.

As at most bars I know, my regulars are mostly men. And
they're a good crew: cabinetmakers, chefs, painters, teachers,
other bartenders, and freelancers of many stripes. I love my
day drinkers: Since they work unorthodox hours, they can
come to the bar when others can't. During the day, it seldom
gets too loud or too crowded. We talk, we toast, we catch up
on one another's news, lives, families. Every now and then,
when I have to take a Tuesday off, I miss seeing them. When
I tell them that, some seem to think I'm trying to flatter them,
but it's the truth.

Observing my customers over on the civilian side of the bar often gives me the uncanny feeling that I'm watching a film about my own life, even if I'm just out of frame. I see people falling in love with this bar, as I fell in love with so many other bars. I see how it happens and the way it takes hold: First they're in once a month, then twice, then every week. Even if they're a little shy at first, all it takes is a good conversation with the person sitting on the next barstool (or with the person behind the bar) to feel fully at ease. It has become a second home for them, as Puffy's and Good World and Grogan's and other bars once were for me. They come alone. They come with friends and coworkers, and sometimes even their wives and adult children. They come in good moods and celebrate, and in bad moods to drink away their troubles. This is *their* community center. This is their local. And just as so many bartenders became my friends over the years, I've become their friend, too.

And of course I can't help paying closest attention to the women who drink here, especially those who are regulars and, among them, those who are young and single and come on their own. The lives of a few seem to revolve around this little bar. This is where they've made their closest friends. Sometimes, I see them elsewhere in the neighborhood. When I do, they are often with people they met at the bar, not infrequently members of its staff. And I feel like I'm having a flashback. They remind me more than a little of someone I knew years ago. Recently, I noticed one woman coming in from time to time with a friend. Then she started coming on her own. She'd take a seat at the end of the bar near the door, drink beer, and knit. She has told me how much she likes the bar, how comfortable she feels there, how much it reminds her of warm, unpretentious places in her hometown. By now, many of the regulars know her by name, and the knitting needles and yarn come out less often. When I see her, I remember grading papers at Puffy's Tavern, ensconced in one of those booths, drinking Guinness, occasionally listening in on conversations among the regulars—and then becoming one of them.

Like me, the women who are regulars at my bar love to drink. At a bar. In the company of men. There are moments when I want to protect them if it looks like they're about to make a familiar misstep: go home with someone not quite worthy of their affection, confide in someone who might not be trustworthy, drink one too many. But I can't intervene too much, and I think they're getting as much out of this kind of life as I once did. Being a woman at home in bar culture is a way of figuring out who you are, and of getting comfortable with her. It's an assertion of independence. I'd be the last person to get in the way.

ACKNOWLEDGMENTS

Not long after I started writing this book, my husband, Frank Duba, was diagnosed with cancer. He faced it with extraordinary grace until his death in 2010. At the time of his diagnosis, we were separated; love and circumstances unseparated us. This was a story I could not tell here, but Frank is present on every page, and no words of appreciation or affection could ever suffice.

I'm grateful for my painstaking and patient editor, Megan Lynch, who rescued me from many of my worst impulses, her wonderful assistant, Alexandra Cardia, and publisher Geoffrey Kloske at Riverhead; for my coolheaded agent, Scott Waxman, and his associates; and for Ira Glass, Julie Snyder, and their colleagues at *This American Life*, which aired an early version of this book's first chapter, setting the whole thing in motion.

I'm indebted to Catherine Gilbert Murdock, the author of the excellent book *Domesticating Drink,* who gamely and graciously answered my questions about women and bar culture before Prohibition and directed me to other helpful resources.

My dear brother, Jeremy Schaap, supported and encouraged me immeasurably. Among my beloved friends, I especially thank Elena Alexander, Jami Attenberg, John Bowman, Philip Casey, Jiwon Choi, Andy Kolovos, Lisa Ng, Dael Orlandersmith, John

Paul, Lu Ratunil, Michael Sharkey, Ann Shostrom, Geoffrey Smyth, Annika Sundvik, and Jeffrey Walkowiak.

And: Anaheed Alani, Michael Andre, Jeff Baker, Matthew Beckerman, Claire Birmingham, Susan Black, Carla Bolte, Lex Braes, Dee Byrd-Molnar and Paul Molnar, Kate Christensen, Andrew Cohen, Wyn Cooper, T. L. Cowan, Brian Currid, Jennifer Dickinson, Susan Dumois, Aylin Emeksiz, Dori Fern, Brendan Fitzgerald, Roland Gebhardt, Benjamin Gervis, Dan Gillham, Jeff Gordinier, Sophie Gorlin, Teri Greeves, Dave Guimond, Rick Hamlin, Anthony Hauck, Debbie Hecht, Ken Heitmueller, Vivian Heller, Jean Holabird, Sylvia and Bob Jorlett, Blaise Kearsley, Bernice and Paul Kelly, Jon Kelly, Max Langrind, Katherine Lanpher, John Lavelle, Hugo Lindgren, Howard McCalebb, Brian McNally, Andra Miller, Reggie Miller, Meredith Morton, Joe Mueller, Sarah Nankin, Maud Newton, Eustace Pilgrim, Jasmine Rault, Angus Robertson, Roots Café, Maria and John Ross, Maura Spiegel, John Stoate, Ruth Sullivan, Mark Sweeney, Josephine Vazquez, Wilhelm Werthern, Craig West, Charles Yoder, Maggie Zackheim, Jenny Zeuli, Susan Zugaib, I raise a glass to you all—*sláinte, skål, salut, na zdrowie, prost, cheers.*

Rosie Schaap has been a bartender, a fortune-teller, a librarian at a paranormal society, an English teacher, an editor, a preacher, a community organizer, and a manager of homeless shelters. A contributor to *This American Life* and NPR.org, she writes the "Drink" column for the *New York Times Magazine.* She was born in New York City and still lives there.